Copyright © 2023 Leadership Reno, LLC. All rights reserved.

Published by Leadership Reno, LLC. Atlanta, Georgia.

No part of this book may be reproduced, or stored in a retrieval system, or transmitted in any form or by any means, electronic, mechanical, photocopying, recording, or otherwise, except as permitted under Section 107 or 108 of the 1976 United States Copyright Act, without express written permission of the publisher.

While the publisher and author have used their best efforts in preparing this book, they make no representations or warranties with respect to the accuracy or completeness of the contents of this book and specifically disclaim any implied warranties of merchantability or fitness for a particular purpose. No warranty may be created or extended by sales representatives or written sales materials. The advice and strategies contained herein may not be suitable for your situation. You should consult with a professional where appropriate. Furthermore, readers should be aware that websites and resources listed in this work may have changed disappeared since this book was written. Neither the publisher nor author should be libel for any loss of profit or any other commercial damages, including but not limited to, special, incidental, consequential, or other damages.

ISBN: 979-8-9890034-0-2 (ebook)
ISBN: 979-8-9890034-1-9 (paperback)
ISBN: 979-8-9890034-2-6 (hardback)

Cover design: Lisa Edmondson
Author photo: Jennifer Yench and Boomer

Printed in the United States of America

◆◆◆

A former employee once told me that they think I'm such a great leader *because* I'm a mom.

This book is dedicated to my children, Hadley, and Noah.
Being your mother was my first and best lesson in leadership. Thank you for reminding me daily what really matters… and for inspiring me to be a better person and leader.

◆◆◆

Contents

Important Note About This Book 8
PREFACE 9
CHAPTER 1: THE "WHY" OF IT ALL 11
    Employee Engagement and People Leaders 13
    Why Do I Care? 19
    The Impetus for a Book 22
    The Inspiration for this Book 23
    Why Ethology? 28
    TL;DR Chapter 1: The "Why" of It All 30
CHAPTER 2: THE CORPORATE PEACOCK 31
    About the Peacock 32
    Executive Presence, Imposter Syndrome, & the Corporate Peacock .. 34
    Corporate Peacocks & The Corporate Ladder 38
    The Culpability of the C-Suite 40
    Characteristics of a Corporate Peacock / Toxic Boss 43
    TL; DR Chapter 2: The Corporate Peacock 45
CHAPTER 3: THE CARDINAL AS G.O.A.T. 46
    About the Cardinal 47
    Leadership Lessons from the Cardinal 49
    Differentiating the CARDINAL Leader 50
    Measuring the CARDINAL Leader 52

Characteristics of the CARDINAL Leader 54

TL; DR Chapter 3: The Cardinal as G.O.A.T. 58

CHAPTER 4: HUMILITY & THE WOLF 60

About the Wolf 61

Leadership Lessons in Humility from the Wolf 62

Interviewing for Humility 64

TL; DR Chapter 4: Humility & the Wolf 66

CHAPTER 5: HONESTY & THE SWAN 68

About the Swan 69

Leadership Lessons in Honesty from the Swan 71

Interviewing for Honesty 74

TL; DR Chapter 5: Honesty & the Swan 76

CHAPTER 6: AUTHENTICITY & THE DOG 77

About the Dog 78

Leadership Lessons in Authenticity from the Dog 79

Interviewing for Authenticity 82

TL; DR Chapter 6: Authenticity & the Dog 84

CHAPTER 7: INSPIRATION & THE LION 86

About the Lion 87

Leadership Lessons in Inspiration from the Lion 88

Interviewing for Inspiration 91

TL; DR Chapter 7: Inspiration & the Lion 95

CHAPTER 8: SELFLESSNESS & THE GORILLA 97
About the Gorilla 99
Leadership Lessons in Selflessness from the Gorilla 100
Interviewing for Selflessness 102
TL; DR Chapter 8: Selflessness & the Gorilla 105

CHAPTER 9: EMPATHY & THE ELEPHANT 106
About the Elephant 107
Leadership Lessons in Empathy from the Elephant 108
Interviewing for Empathy 111
TL; DR Chapter 9: Empathy & the Elephant 113

CHAPTER 10: YOUR ACTION PLAN FOR LEADERSHIP REFORM 115
Ground Zero: Establish Your Pack by Starting at the Top 116
    My Leadership Reform Pack Members 117
Step 1: Implement Employee Engagement Surveys 127
Step 2: Modify Your Standards for Hiring People Leaders 130
Step 3: Revise the Performance Metrics for your People Leaders ... 131
Step 4: Rehome, Rehabilitate or Retrain your Toxic Bosses 133
TL; DR Chapter 10: Your Action Plan for Leadership Reform 135

CONCLUSION 136
About The Author 138
Acknowledgements 139
Endnotes 142

Important Note About This Book

For my fellow ADHD'ers, I have included a "TL; DR" section at the end of each chapter. Most of you know this is social media speak for "Too Long; Didn't Read." It's basically a bullet-point formatted recap of the longer, preceding text in each chapter. So, there's no excuse for you not to finish this book and help change the world with Leadership Reform! You're welcome.

Lisa

◆ ◆ ◆

PREFACE

"Let us not forget that human love and compassion are equally deeply rooted in our primate heritage."

– Dr. Jane Goodall -- Ethologist, Primatologist, Conservationist

I began writing this book knowing there were literally hundreds and hundreds of great books about leadership already on the market. Over a dozen of which I added to my personal library over a decade ago when I was researching and designing a Leadership Development curriculum for the company I worked for at the time. One thing they all seemed to have in common is—THEY'RE ALL COMMON SENSE! Why would I want to "throw my hat into the ring" in an already saturated market? And if I did, why would my book be any different? How could I approach this subject in a way that helped people and made them want to read my book?

I was a successful leader of a high-performing team who had unfortunately fallen under the direction of a toxic boss and had been subsequently laid off from a job that I held for a decade. Therefore, I had first-hand experience with the amazing things that a team could do when they had a GREAT leader in place. I had also gained first-hand experience of the devastation a toxic boss could do to that same team.

The traumatic experience of being laid off by a toxic boss prompted me to want to help others in similar scenarios. So, off I went to the internet. I was astonished to learn that there already was a whole robust industry in place that dealt with every aspect of "workplace bullying." From coaching firms to professional counseling organizations to legal resources. Wonderful people fighting every day to help people like me who had been a target of bullying at work. I learned a lot about workplace bullying, including how to stand up for myself if I ever experienced that type of scenario again. Based on my findings, I created a Telly Award-winning training video on the topic, which I've made available for free on my YouTube channel. More on that later.

I guess it's a good thing that I wasn't already an "expert" on workplace bullying. I feel fortunate that I'd been in the workforce almost three decades before I personally had to deal with it. I was astonished to learn of the overwhelming prevalence of workplace bullying and toxic bosses in organizations across the globe. I couldn't help but question, "How are people like that consistently placed in positions of leadership?" and "How can we prevent that from continuing to happen?"

So, while I didn't have a lot of experience with bullying, I had an abundance of experience with leadership. And based on my leadership experience, I knew that if an organization had the right people leaders in place, workplace bullying could become obsolete.

This book is my answer to why there are so many toxic bosses in the workplace and what people and organizations can do to ingratiate the right kind of leaders back into the workforce. The cost of not doing so is detrimental to our society and economy. In short:

We need to redefine the metrics we use to hire, measure, and select people leaders across the globe.

WE NEED LEADERSHIP REFORM!

◆◆◆

CHAPTER 1: THE "WHY" OF IT ALL

$8.8 trillion dollars!!

That's a huge freaking number! It's impossible to fathom that amount of money. I might as well have said "eleventy billion dollars."

Yet even though that sounds like an imaginary number, it's actually the figure Gallup provided in their 2023 State of the Global Workplace report[i] to describe the cost of low employee engagement to the global economy. And that number represents an **increase** of 2% from the prior year in employee engagement worldwide, reaching a record high of 23% since the pandemic. Yay for mediocrity!

Gallup's definition of employee engagement is, "the involvement and enthusiasm of employees in both their work and workplace." Why does employee engagement matter? Simply stated, Gallup further explains that **"highly engaged teams outperform the rest** in business outcomes critical to the success of your organization."

Employee Engagement

Definition: The involvement and enthusiasm of employees in both their work and workplace.

Shameful plug for Gallup, "a global analytics and advice firm that helps leaders and organizations solve their most pressing problems."

Figure 1-1: From "Leadership Reno: Transforming your Business by Putting More Women in Charge," a.k.a. "[How to Select People Leaders Who Will Drive Your Business Forward](#)" available at [www.leadershipreno.com](#) and [youtube.com/@thediyleader](#).

Business outcomes include those that result in increased productivity and profits. So, if highly engaged teams "outperform the rest in business outcomes critical to the success of your organization," logic would suggest that we would all want more of this magical thing called employee engagement. So, how do organizations increase employee engagement? Ironically, the answer is less complex than you would think, and it doesn't include advanced business degrees, state-of-the-art technology or even a magical formula to achieve. Quite simply... the answer to increased employee engagement and therefore increased productivity and profits is having the right PEOPLE LEADERS in place. Period. Oh, and a happy side effect of having the right people leaders in place is the eradication of toxic bosses and workplace bullying. Double-bonus points!

◆◆◆

Employee Engagement and People Leaders

Let's explore further this concept of people leaders, employee engagement, and profitability. This article from the University of Oxford[ii] states that research by Oxford University's Saïd Business School, in collaboration with British multinational telecoms firm BT, found a conclusive link between employee happiness and productivity. Their extensive study found that workers are 13% more productive when happy. Taking into consideration factors such as pay, weather, vacation, and even the number of windows in the office, the common "happiness factor" is attributed to "managerial practices."

Not only that, but I also knew from over a decade of personal experience as a people leader that employee engagement was fundamental to the performance of the team. High employee engagement equated to happy employees. Happy employees equated to a high-performing team. A high-performing team equated to a productive team. And by default, a productive team equated to a profitable team.

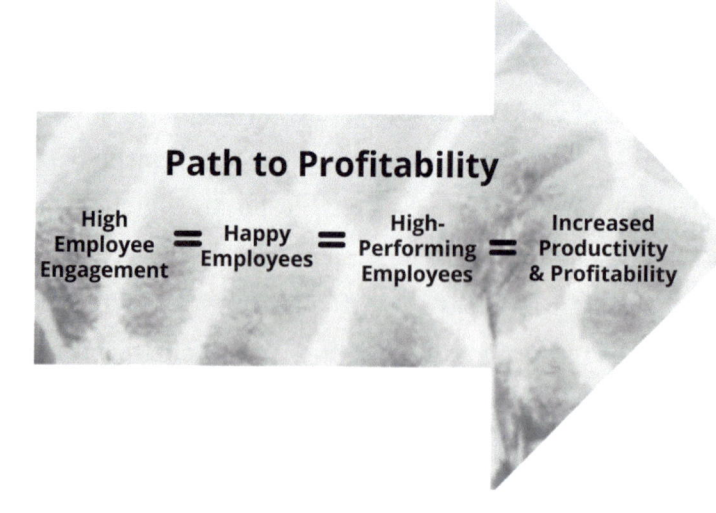

Path to Profitability

High Employee Engagement = Happy Employees = High-Performing Employees = Increased Productivity & Profitability

In every poll/scenario/report that measures the health of an organization, you'll find a direct correlation between employee engagement scores and the performance of the organization. Once again, I defer to the empirical data resulting from Gallup's meta-analysis research. Here are the findings from their most recent study, done in 2020 (Gallup 2023)[iii]:

> In 2020, Gallup conducted its 10th meta-analysis on the Q^{12} using 456 research studies across 276 organizations in 54 industries and 96 countries. Within each study, Gallup researchers statistically calculated the work-unit-level relationship between employee engagement and performance outcomes that the organization supplied. Researchers studied 112,312 work units, including 2.7 million employees. This 10th iteration of the meta-analysis further confirmed the well-established connection between employee engagement and 11 performance outcomes:
>
> - customer loyalty/engagement
> - profitability
> - productivity
> - turnover (for high-turnover and low-turnover organizations)
> - safety incidents
> - shrinkage (theft)
> - absenteeism
> - patient safety incidents
> - quality (defects)
> - wellbeing (net thriving employees)
> - organizational citizenship (participation)

Figure 1-2: From "The Benefits of Employee Engagement" by Gallup.

Gallup further emphasizes that "employee engagement and wellbeing are reciprocal and additive" and that **companies with engaged employees also have higher earnings per share with publicly traded companies**. Again… hard evidence to support the significance of and link between employee engagement surveys and company performance.

If you haven't taken part in an employee engagement survey before, the recommended practice is to conduct these surveys annually via a non-partial, reputable 3rd party (reputable is the key here to ensure the 3rd party isn't influenced by the company signing the bill). These surveys are answered anonymously by employees and typically consist of anywhere between 50 to 100 questions that pertain specifically to their organization. Engagement surveys are designed to measure how invested or "connected" employees feel towards their work and the organization as whole. Represented on a scale of 0 to 100, employee engagement surveys measure employees' "favorable" or "unfavorable" opinions of their organization in categories such as:

- Job Opportunities
- Company Culture
- Company Leadership
- My Work
- Resources & Teamwork
- Net Promotor Score (How likely the employee is to continue working with the organization, whether they would recommend their organization to a family member or friend, etc.)
- My Manager

It's not unusual for a company's target score on these surveys to be somewhere in the 60% or 70% range overall. Over the years that I led a team at a company that conducted employee engagement surveys, my personal scores in the **My Manager** category were always in the 80s and 90s. Year after year. Even more telling were the scores from those same employees in the categories that I had no control over. For example, Net Promoter Score, Company Leadership and Company Culture scores from my employees were consistently in the 30s, 40s and 50s at the same time they were ranking me in the 80s and 90s.

Knowing the categories that are typically measured in employee engagement surveys, it's no surprise that these scores **decreased** across-the-board during the pandemic. COVID-19 forced people to recognize the fragility of life and reevaluate what's important to them. Not surprisingly, the overwhelming conclusion was that work was not as big of a priority as they had originally assumed. So, employees quit their jobs. Many even switched careers during the pandemic. This mass exodus, known as "The Great Resignation," had two key motivating factors:

1. Reprioritization of personal priorities due to the pandemic, and
2. Broader job options due to newly available remote work opportunities

Millions and millions of people who never thought it was possible to work from home suddenly found themselves in that very scenario. And they LOVED it. Not only did they love it, but they demanded it from their employers. With remote work options opening the doors to a global job market where anyone with a computer and the right skills could now get a job almost anywhere in the world, organizations were suddenly put in a position where *they had to compete* for top talent just as much as job seekers had to compete for remote work options!

---

*Organizations were suddenly competing for top talent **just as much as** job seekers were competing for remote work options!*

Of course, pay is always a factor for job seekers, especially when the average pay raise is not keeping up with the cost of living. However, happy, engaged employees place much less importance on pay, as compared to other factors such as remote work flexibility and having a great leader. Additionally, happy employees don't bully. Therefore, when you boil down the data to why some companies have an advantage over others, one key factor was not more pay or job opportunities, but rather, the company culture and their leaders! Suddenly people leaders became the "secret weapon" of employers to win over top talent.

In the Gallup State of the Workplace survey mentioned previously, Gallup estimates the following:

> *Managers account for "at least 70% of the variance in employee engagement scores across business units."*
>
> *This means employee motivation is often made or broken through their managers.*

If your organization has great people leaders already in place, then you are ahead of the pack. Sadly, this new global job market further highlights the ongoing matter of poor leaders and toxic bosses. People no longer have to "just deal with" toxic bosses anymore. So, they don't.

Turns out... the pandemic also brought to light the workforces' dirty little secret... there are a ton of inferior people leaders out there! Companies can no longer hide the fact that they have toxic bosses in their organization. Just check out the reviews for any company on www.glassdoor.com and you won't have to look far to locate a poor review provided by a disgruntled former employee lamenting the subpar leadership or toxic boss they were all too happy to escape. And when there is one complaint of this nature, there are often many more that follow.

Toxic bosses aren't selective. Therefore, if they have more than one employee, there's a strong probability that their toxicity is water-cooler talk amongst their employees. While some employees are able to keep a low profile and stay off the toxic boss's radar, the mere fact that they're avoiding that "radar" is clear evidence that they are aware that their boss is toxic. They're also probably thankful that they're not the target of his/her bullying. The fact there is a large population of people who just have to "deal with a toxic boss" is unacceptable and should anger anyone reading this. Why is this tolerated?

That's not to say that toxic bosses are a new thing in the workforce. They've always been around. The Second World War is a primary example of the most extreme version of how a single, toxic boss can devastate entire populations and countries. While hundreds of thousands of people voluntarily followed the lead of that one person, I challenge you to consider what our world would look like today if there had never been a Hitler, or a Holocaust. The lessons we learned from that dark period in our history are lessons that should not go to waste. I know my family tree would be significantly more robust if there had not been a Hitler.

My point is this— employees now have alternatives. The ripple effect poor leaders can have on organizations and society, in general, is so far reaching it's incalculable. So those organizations who don't address the toxic bosses in their organization who are directly responsible for low employee engagement scores <u>will</u> get left behind.

The amazing thing is that the opposite is true as well. The positive ripple effect GREAT leaders have on organizations and society is tangible and measurable, with employee engagement surveys providing a clear picture in that regard. Therefore, it's imperative that we do everything we can to ensure that the "ripples" are positive, rather than negative... and that starts with global Leadership Reform in the workplace.

◆◆◆

Why Do I Care?

I have extensive experience as a people leader. Not just any people leader, but a successful people leader. How do I know this? My employees told me so. That, alone, makes me a credible authority on leadership. My record of 0% employee turnover during my 10 years as a people leader in one organization is further proof that I was a great leader. If you don't appreciate the significance of that number, let me spell it out for you.

Gallup estimates turnover to equal 1/3 of payroll each year[iv]. Let's assume I had 15 employees whose average salary was $90,000 annually:

- 90,000 x 15 = $450,000 in payroll / year
- 1/3 of $450,000 = $150,000 / year
- $150,000 x 10 years = $1.5 million dollars

I saved my company over a million dollars by literally doing nothing more than treating my employees humanely. Additionally, in 2022, the government established a "reward" for certain organizations that experienced 0% turnover during COVID-19, specifically the time frame from October 2020 to November 2021. I know there are certain stipulations that qualify a company for this stipend. However, I think it's notable that the stipend the government was offering was $26,000 per employee. Therefore, in my case:

- $26,000 x 15 = $390,000

If my company qualified for this stipend, I would have actually EARNED almost $400,000 for my company during a year when employee turnover reached an all-time high across the globe. Point being... even the government recognizes the significance of low employee turnover.

Compared to the [2021 Bureau of Labor Statistics Report](#) rate of 57.3% for overall employee turnover, that clearly puts me in the "above average" category of people managers. Add to that the numerous accolades my employees consistently provided for me via internal recognition applications and social media networks, I'd say we had something magical occurring *especially* during the time of the pandemic and the Great Resignation. The honor of leading them motivated me every day to show up and do MY best for them. It takes a special kind of person to be a successful people leader. Many folks just aren't cut out for the role. And many are not only NOT cut out for the role, but they seem to fall into that NSFW (Not Safe for Work) category. They're quite literally toxic!

For those sports fans out there, I bet you can personally name at least 2 or 3 college or professional teams where the team members may fluctuate; however, with the right coach in place, they consistently win College Championships or Super Bowls year after year. Or, in the music industry, you hear of those "unicorn" partnerships with artists such as Elton John and Bernie Taupin, or Steven Tyler and Joe Perry of Aerosmith, or Machine Gun Kelly and Travis Barker (for any millennials in the crowd). Sometimes the stars align, and the right people happen to be in the right place at the right time, and magic ensues. That same chemistry can be achieved in the corporate world as well when you have the right leaders in place. Great leaders, like great coaches, can *create* magic with their team. In my case, I led with a "people first" mentality, and that meant:

- Trusting my employees to do their jobs
- Delegating projects to them to align with their strengths and develop their skills

- Empowering them to make decisions on their own
- Being humble, transparent, and honest
- Maintaining open lines of communication, including monthly team calls, newsletters, a team SharePoint site, and regular 1-on-1 calls
- Frequently procuring their input for improvements, and then listening to and incorporating their suggestions
- Offering tough love to fairly mitigate the occasional disagreement, if needed

The result was a highly productive team of engaged, innovative individuals who were fiercely loyal to me. We were a well-oiled machine creating transformative work and just "making great music together" that resulted in big profits for the organization. What more could you ask for?

◆◆◆

The Impetus for a Book

A change in leadership in my department brought that well-oiled machine to its knees. Enter… the toxic boss who saw me as a threat. Suddenly, I was "incompetent" and couldn't do anything right. The emojis in my emails were offensive and I was too transparent with my team according to this new leadership. The bullying and harassment I endured lasted for 6 months before I was fired from a job where my team was a top producer, and I was revered by my employees. As mentioned previously, that experience launched my journey of discovery to better understand why I was targeted by my bullies, and to identify how I could prevent others from going through what I did.

I spent the next year creating my own LLC, conducting intense research daily, hosting podcasts, participating in podcasts, and networking with dozens and dozens of experts in the field to "find the answer for dealing with bullies" and the "solution for toxic leaders." The result was an eLearning curriculum that I created based on the works of John Lenhart of www.flowcess.com (for bullying) and Dr. Tomas Chamorro-Premuzic, author, TEDx Talk presenter and Chief Innovation Officer of The Manpower Group (for Leadership). More on these two later.

I've made all of that content available for free on my website at www.leadershipreno.com and YouTube channel at www.youtube.com/@thediyleader.

I'm proud to say that one of my videos won a **Silver Telly Award** in 2023 in the category of **Social Video > General – Workplace Culture**. That award further validated my expertise in the L&D space, and more importantly, the dire need for a solution to workplace bullying and toxic leaders.

❖❖❖

The Inspiration for this Book

I'm an animal lover and confess that most days, I like animals more than people. However, it's the empathy that I feel for animals that also makes me a better people leader. Let me share with you the true story that prompted me to look to the animal kingdom as inspiration for this book.

On an ordinary sunny Saturday in August, I entered my garage to hop in my car for a quick run to the store. As soon as I exited the house into the garage, I saw a female cardinal flying around within the vaulted ceiling of our garage. I don't know how long she had been there. We have a 2-door garage, and both garage doors were open at that time. Therefore, I figured I'd just stand still for a few minutes until she exited through one of the open garage doors.

I watched her fly from the top of one open garage door to the top of the other open garage door. Then she'd flutter around and land on one of the garage door opener mechanisms that was bolted to the roof of the garage. She did this numerous times and from my perspective, seemed to be a little panicked. After watching her do this for a few minutes, I then started to panic because I realized that, for whatever reason, she couldn't seem to fly low enough to escape out the open door to freedom. She kept fluttering around in the roof area of the garage.

Of course, "shooing her out with a broom" was not even remotely an option for me. So, instead I ran out the garage door into the driveway in hopes that me being out of her line of sight would help her feel less panicked and she'd find her way out. Still nothing. She continued flying around in the ceiling of the garage. Of course, I then tried to "call her out" of the garage. Many animals are known for their intelligence. It's been demonstrated time and time again. So, my logic was that maybe she would hear my voice and understand which way was "out." Even then, she still would only fly from the top of one garage door to the other. I think she even tired herself out. Because at one point, she landed on top of one of the open garage doors and stayed there. I took that opportunity to run back into the garage and pull my car out, thinking the open bay and open space would make her exit path to freedom more obvious.

Yet she still fluttered around in the roof of the garage. I then pulled my car out into the street, thinking one last time that my presence must have her afraid to fly out of the garage. So, I sat in my car in the street, well away from the garage, believing I'd see her fly out any minute. What I saw instead was her male partner, frantically flying around outside of the garage.

At first, it seemed his lingering was just instinctual. I figured he's thinking, "The kids are hungry. Stop messing around in this garage and get home to feed the kids because I'm going to hang out with the boys." And then I expected to see him fly off. (I said I was an animal lover; not an expert). But after a while, I could tell his efforts were more than instinctual, because he wouldn't leave. His behavior indicated he was more invested in her than just "get home and feed the kids."

I watched him as he evaluated the situation. I first noticed him when he landed on the car in the driveway that was parked outside the open garage door. Then he landed on the ground outside the garage door and walked up closer to the garage opening. Then he perched on the flood lights outside the garage door. Next, he flew into the garage and back out again.

That's when I lost it. (Seriously, tearing up now as well). It was so sad to watch his flurry of (what I can only interpret as) "panic," trying everything possible to help her. With tears running down my face, I got out of my car and went back into the garage to get my husband to come outside and see if he could help. However, when I got inside the garage, he was already standing there, watching her. I told him about the male hovering outside the garage. He could tell I was upset. Thankfully, he's an animal lover too, so I knew he wouldn't walk away until she got out. Only then was I able to get back in my car and proceed with my errand.

When I got home from the store less than an hour later, he told me the story of how she finally landed on a shelf inside the garage, then landed on the ground in the vacated space where my car was previously parked, then flew out. I was so relieved to know that she had gotten out. Standing in the "box" that was my garage, I immediately thought back to a conversation I had just had with a friend of mine the day before. She's writing a memoir about how she struggled her entire life with people trying to "put her in a box." That's when I broke down, again. Thinking of that poor little cardinal being stuck in the "box" of our garage.

No one deserves to be put in a box. No one. Not even animals. Of course, for the cardinal, her partner's loyalty was that of a marine. He clearly was NOT going to leave her behind.

Then I thought, "Why can't humans be more like those cardinals? Why isn't our instinct to always want to help others find their way out of the box? Why don't we all exhaust ourselves trying to help others break free from whatever is holding them back? Why is the human race so indifferent to toxic bosses that they're allowed to continue to manage other humans?" (ADHD brain... remember?)

Figure 1-3: Male cardinal on floodlight above garage.

Figures 1-4 and 1-5: Male cardinal on ground outside of garage.

Click. Click. Click. The synapses in my brain finally started firing and 20 minutes later, I had found the inspiration to get beyond my "writer's block" with this book and subsequently had written and posted "The Cardinal Story" on a social media site. I then spent the remainder of the weekend researching (ok... googling) "animal behavior" and "leadership in animals," looking to the animal kingdom for examples of leadership that I could reference for this book. The more I learned, the more I realized how much stronger leadership skills are in the animal kingdom. And that we could learn a lot from animals.

◆◆◆

Why Ethology?

Why not? Through my research, I was reminded that the study of animal behavior is known as ethology. This book is a study in leadership behavior. Therefore, it seemed appropriate.

Dr. Jane Goodall is probably the most recognizable ethologist of our time, with her lifelong study of natural behaviors of the chimpanzees of Tanzania. Based on my research, two key observations I noted as an "armchair ethologist" of leaders:

- Like humans, animals are known to have both instinctual behavior and learned behavior. These behaviors are exactly as you would expect: Instinctual behavior is inherited or visceral (like that "gut" feeling in humans), and learned behavior is learned and developed throughout their lifetime.
- There is no "standard" across species of how the leaders of each group are determined.

The result: I knew how to fix the problem companies were facing worldwide with poor productivity, poor leaders, and costly employee turnover. Combine that with the inspiration I gained from the animal kingdom, and you have my atypical approach to Leadership Reform in the workplace.

In this book, I'll share with you some relatable, yet fundamental, tips to implement Leadership Reform in your organization. I'll describe the characteristics we should be looking for when hiring, promoting, and evaluating people leaders. I'll also explore the consequences of not making Leadership Reform a priority in your organization. And lastly, I'll provide you with a high-level action plan for implementing Leadership Reform in your workplace.

If nothing else, simply reducing turnover in your organization can save you millions of dollars in payroll and turnover costs each year. That alone seems like it would be worth your while to "give us a read".

◆◆◆

TL;DR Chapter 1: The "Why" of It All

- Employee engagement is a direct indicator of productivity.
- Productivity is a direct indicator of company performance.
- Managers are the #1 influencer on whether employees feel engaged.
- We need better people leaders in the workplace.
- We need Leadership Reform.

◆◆◆

CHAPTER 2: THE CORPORATE PEACOCK

"I suppose I always thought — better to be a fake somebody than a real nobody."

-- Tom Ripley – from "The Talented Mr. Ripley"

Before I get into what we SHOULD be looking for in our people leaders, I need to paint a picture of the type of toxic bosses that are currently way too prevalent in the workforce and why we need Leadership Reform to rehabilitate, eradicate, or replace them. Subsequent chapters in this book will go into immense detail of the characteristics we should be looking for. But first, I felt it was imperative to elaborate on the "Glamour Don't" before getting into the "Glamour Do" of leadership.

When it comes to the animal kingdom, I'd have to say there's no greater example of a toxic boss than the peacock. Sadly, a large majority of toxic bosses are narcissists. So, it seemed appropriate to pontificate about the peacock a bit to further illustrate what NOT to look for when filling leadership roles and explain why this particular phenomenon persists in our supposedly advanced society.

◆◆◆

About the Peacock

I have always been fascinated by peacocks. They are absolutely stunning creatures whose amazing plume of feathers is one of the most beautiful things I have ever seen in nature. Erm well... at the zoo. That is until I finally did see some in nature.

My husband and I were driving around looking at houses out in the more suburban areas of Atlanta, and we ran across a farm that had at least a dozen peacocks, just roaming around freely. I made my husband pull over to the side of the road so that I could take pictures. I had never seen a peacock outside of the zoo, so I was even further mesmerized when I got to observe them in their "natural habitat." Seeing a peacock perched in a tree, on the roof of a barn or on a split-rail fence was to me like witnessing a phenomenon. Nothing impressive, as peacocks can fly. But the sight was so unusual to me that it did seem like I was witnessing a miracle. Their feathers and coloring are so stunning that I felt compelled to include them on the cover of this book.

So, why do peacocks get an entire chapter? During my weekend of being an "armchair ethologist," I learned that peacocks are basically asses. Well, not literally. But as soon as I read about their characteristics, I knew immediately that I had found my "narcissist" of the animal kingdom and for this book. A little bit about peacocks:

- Peacocks are the male variety of the species. There are no female peacocks.
- You don't refer to peacocks as "male peacocks." That's like saying a "male man."
- The female of this species is called a peahen.
- Together, they are generically referred to as "peafowl."

- A group of peafowl is called an "ostentation," "muster," "party" or "pride." (the human declaration of animal group names is often a reference from some trait or personality of the animal).
- Peacocks are the only members of the species who have the impressive coloring and plumage we all think of when we think of the peafowl.
- The poor peahens, on the other hand, do NOT have that huge plumage of tail feathers, nor do they have that remarkable blue/green coloring all over their body. The little peahen typically has a soft-brown, chestnut-colored body with a little blue/green coloring on her neck. She also has a lovely brown or rust-colored head.
- Peacocks are polygamous, displaying no loyalty to or connection with a single female. They mate with multiple females throughout their lifespan and use their beautiful array of feathers for nothing more than impressing the chicks…er, peahens.
- Once the peacock mates with the peahen, he doesn't even stick around for a cigarette or a cuddle. He goes back to hanging out with the boys, leaving the peahen to incubate the eggs (about 30 days) and raise the chicks on her own when they hatch.
- The peacock's call is unique and loud (and annoying, IMO). You always know when you are in the presence of a peacock.

◆◆◆

Executive Presence, Imposter Syndrome, & the Corporate Peacock

One other important thing to note about our narcissistic, corporate peacock toxic boss is that they are masters of the game when it comes to exhibiting executive presence! I wanted to spend some time discussing this concept, because I believe the corporate peacock's ability to display executive presence is why they are able to continue to move up the corporate ladder.

Not surprisingly, I learned about "executive presence" from one of my bullies. Here I had been successfully leading a team of employees for a decade, and suddenly, I needed to work on my "executive presence." So, I looked it up. At the time, and still today, the term "executive presence" does not exist in Webster's dictionary. I'm sure it will only be a matter of time before it does appear. But it hasn't made the list yet.

I did stumble across this [Forbes article](#)[v] from 2018, though, that defines executive presence as "your ability to inspire confidence — inspiring confidence in your subordinates that you're the leader they want to follow, inspiring confidence among peers that you're capable and reliable and, most importantly, inspiring confidence among senior leaders that you have the potential for great achievements."

Here is where I need to make a distinction between those who have actual executive presence and those who simply know how to mimic executive presence. Remember, our corporate peacocks are self-serving narcissists who manipulate situations with their extraordinary display of feathers. Likewise, our corporate peacocks are IMPOSTERS. How do I know this? Because they do not fit the definition of executive presence as provided previously by Forbes.

When it comes to our corporate peacocks, they do a great job of impressing senior leaders with their executive presence. However, when it comes to their own employees, this is where the corporate peacock reveals himself as an imposter. Imposters do NOT "inspire confidence in their subordinates that they're the leader they want to follow." Employees are smarter than that. By working with their leaders daily, they see through the peacock's display of wisdom and charisma and reserve their respect instead for visionary leaders with a clear direction, good decision-making skills, and a rational demeanor.

Sadly, senior leaders don't really have time to get to know every leader at a deep level. Therefore, they often form their opinion of people based on their executive presence. So, if you are someone who has an "impressive plume" and knows all the right industry jargon to quote, you will be able to "inspire confidence in senior leaders."

Let me provide an example of a corporate peacock who has mastered the art of "executive presence." Think about how much time senior leaders spend in meetings with the C-Suite. Next, think about how much time they spend to "prepare" for those meetings. In many instances, their "preparation" period is often disproportionate to the amount of time they actually spend with the big guys and girls. Not only that, how often do senior leaders have a team of employees who provide the presentation/content/tools/graphs/data, etc. to the senior leaders in preparation for their time with the C-Suite? You'd think they were preparing to purchase a house with the amount of scurrying around that occurs to provide the corporate peacock with the ammunition they need to have any kind of informative discussion with executives.

Of course, this is merely my opinion, based on my personal observations. I have yet to find anyone who has been able to make a case otherwise, though. I'm not sure if I find it sad, humiliating, satisfying, or a combination of all three, but a key giveaway that you're in the presence of an imposter corporate peacock, is when they mispronounce a word in "their" presentation. Everyone on their team recognizes immediately when a word has been mispronounced. Unfortunately, our corporate peacocks still tend to get away with it when presenting to the C-

Suite, because these mispronounced terms are often new to them as well. Or our corporate peacock has the savvy to "joke it off."

There are a lot of people in high-ranking positions who made it there because they know the art of executive presence, yet they don't actually have the skills to perform the jobs they were hired for. Many folks are catapulted to senior management positions because they are visionaries who have great ideas. Every company needs visionaries. However, the problem comes when that visionary is a corporate peacock who isn't humble enough to admit when they're wrong, admit they don't have all the answers, admit that they aren't always the smartest person in the room and/or that they can learn from their employees.

Executive presence is critical, however, to inspiring confidence in senior leaders. Without it, you will not be welcomed into the "club" (unless you happen to have a personal relationship with the CEO).

The gap between "perceived skills" of a leader and "actual skills" of a leader continues to grow year over year. Imposters have learned that if you can talk the talk, you will be rewarded with promotions and power.

I'm not sure where the actual breaking point is. Somewhere between the C-suite and mid-level management is where you'll find the breeding ground for "imposters with executive presence." This is why it's not uncommon to see some executives job hopping every few years. They may have a vision, but no idea how to execute that vision or even how to predict the outcome of that vision. For many of these imposters, the resulting title, pay, and prestige that go along with it are worth the inconvenience of job hopping and being "found out." Then again... many of these imposters are also narcissistic and therefore genuinely believe their own rhetoric.

To be able to fool hiring executives into thinking that you have the skills for a job simply by having the right "presence" is a skill in and of itself that many have mastered and perfected. They work hard at it. Scientific studies have proven that society tolerates it because our DNA hasn't evolved much in that regard. Historically, a strong, authoritative dictator was necessary for leaders in "ye olde times" when humans were *physically* fighting for control and power. So, even though our subconscious mind still values those traits in leaders; in reality, the actual job requirements for people leaders have changed drastically over the last few centuries. The strong, dictatorial leader needed for battle is no longer the "corporate" version needed for people leaders today.

This 2020 article from comparecamp.com[vi] concludes that the top three leadership performance indicators remain ensconced in the 20th century:

- driving strategy (63%)
- delivering financial results (58%), and
- managing operations well (44%).

This same article also provides overwhelming data that supports the theory that engaged employees are the surefire way for leaders to achieve those top three leadership performance indicators. BUT... to have engaged employees, leaders must exhibit a different set of characteristics that did not make their top three list (transparency, authenticity, humility, honesty, and trust), which we'll discuss later in this book.

Sadly, until our DNA-derived definition of a leader "catches up" with the realistic definition of what's needed in a people leader, "executive presence" will continue to be a deciding factor for leadership roles in the workforce, and we'll continue to see this trend of incompetent people being awarded people leader roles.

◆◆◆

Corporate Peacocks & The Corporate Ladder

Many species in the animal kingdom have gone extinct since the beginning of time. Some went extinct due to catastrophic events of nature, or disease. And some have gone extinct at the hands of humankind, either from hunting or the erosion of the animal's natural habitat due to the expansion of the human race.

Regardless of the economy, people who can work and report to a GREAT Leader will likely stay in their jobs despite what is going on in the world. I've personally seen numerous examples of people who are at or beyond retirement age, yet they continue to work because they enjoy their job, and their leader motivates them to want to continue to work. Unfortunately, many of these GREAT leaders are not the "decision-makers" in the company and are often the first to go when there's a mass layoff. Why is that?

My theory is this: GREAT people leaders seldom make it to the highest executive roles in the corporate world because they are simply not ruthless enough to get there. Their primary concern is not their own status in life. They are not "corporate peacocks" and don't place much importance on executive presence. Instead, they get fulfillment from making genuine connections with their employees, discovering their employees' strengths/what excites them/what makes them tick, and then developing their employees to capitalize on their strengths and reach their goals... cumulatively resulting in a high-performing team.

> *"Great people leaders seldom make it to the highest executive roles in the corporate world, because they are simply not ruthless enough to get there."*
>
> *– Me, The DIY Leader*

As I've stated previously... this is the primary reason why GREAT leaders tend to have unwavering loyalty *from* their employees. And again, this is also the primary reason why senior leaders don't understand the value of these leaders, or why their departments always seem to outperform others.

Senior leaders make the mistake of thinking that these GREAT leaders have high-performing teams simply because they happened to "stumble" across some great employees. It's not until an organization lays off one of these GREAT leaders and their department subsequently stops performing at such a high level (as was the case in the personal scenario I described earlier) that senior leaders MIGHT draw the connection between that GREAT leader they just disposed of, and the decreased performance of their team.

◆◆◆

The Culpability of the C-Suite

Later in this book, I'll provide you with an action plan to implement Leadership Reform at your workplace. You'll find that one of the very first steps to the success of this type of transformation is ensuring that your entire C-Suite is on board with it. For those of you protesting right now with "But it's not their job to worry about all the people leaders within the organization. They have to focus on profits."

Noted!

But as we just proved in Chapter 1 of this book, engaged employees are the path to profits. And people leaders are the conduit to those employees. Smart CEOs know this. Let's look at an all-too-common equivalent scenario from the animal kingdom taking place across the globe.

You know those "big game" hunters whose houses are rife with the heads (and sometimes bodies) of the animals they successfully hunted? Usually they're rich (because big game hunting expeditions require a lot of money... as does taxidermy) and have huge houses that often have entire rooms dedicated to displaying the stuffed trophies of the animals they killed in the wild.

Antelopes, deer, elk, moose, wolves, fox, sheep, and caribou heads are proudly displayed on their walls. Bear, zebra, boar, badger, kangaroo, buffalo, reindeer, and impala rugs line their floors. The list goes on and on. They are proud of their accomplishments and have an impressive story to go along with each one of their conquests.

I see that same type of "trophy mentality" when it comes to the C-Suite assembling their own executive teams at work. Harvard, Yale, Duke, Princeton, Brown, Cornell, and Columbia are some of the Ivy League credentials they prefer to "hang on the walls" when building their executive teams. IBM, Microsoft, Google, 3M, Sony, Intel, Coca-Cola, Disney, and Rolls Royce are some of the credentials they enjoy "carpeting" their executive offices with. Like the big game hunters with their trophy room of exotic stuffed animals, all these credentials (conquests) are self-serving to the "hunter" to make him seem more impressive to others. In other words, within the C-Suite, a primary skillset of their direct reports is often "executive presence." And nothing screams executive presence more than credentials from an Ivy League school or Fortune 100 company.

I'm not saying the C-Suite is full of idiots who have no idea of what's going on with the leaders right beneath their noses. What I am saying is that they often do not place critical importance on the "people side" of the business, but rather are more impressed with the plumes/credentials of their direct reports.

"Dealing with the people side of business is what we have HR for," you might hear some say. Not when it comes to establishing a company culture and selecting other C-Suite candidates and senior leaders. Whether you work for a public company whose CEO answers to a Board of Directors or a private company in which "what the CEO says is law," their go-to preference for their executive team is often a well-publicized corporate peacock with impressive credentials. Or they may opt for a personal recommendation/former colleague/internal promotion from someone on the executive team. In many cases, the C-Suite is focused entirely on credentials when hiring their executive team, and the subsequent sales, revenue, and profits are the measure of that leader.

So, while a toxic boss on the executive team might have 80% turnover, low employee engagement, and even multiple complaints to HR, the "Harvard grad who worked at IBM and looks great on my wall" seems to trump the well-loved "golden retriever" people leader who has high employee engagement and happy, productive employees.

It's not until a leader's sales/revenue/profit numbers begin to drop that the C-Suite takes notice. And why do the toxic bosses sales/revenue/profit numbers always drop? Because they can't do it alone and are often terrible people leaders who can't keep good employees. It's impossible for a people leader to improve their department's productivity when they have a revolving door of employees coming in and going out of their department. And it's impossible for an organization to eradicate toxic bosses in the workplace if the C-Suite doesn't place more importance on the power of its people leaders and the employees who make up the majority of their workforce.

Point being... if there are toxic bosses in your organization, they will continue to prosper if the C-Suite doesn't intervene and take action to reform, eradicate or relocate them. Tolerance or even ignorance of toxic bosses by the C-Suite is equivalent to compliance in this scenario.

◆◆◆

Characteristics of a Corporate Peacock / Toxic Boss

So, let's summarize all the above so that you have a full picture of the type of bosses that need to be eradicated from or rehabilitated within the workforce. You might know a corporate peacock if you work for someone who is:

- Self-centered. Their personal career advancement is their #1 priority, at the expense of everything and everyone else.
- A vocal, charismatic, orator who knows how to draw attention to themselves, even on subjects in which they are not experts.
- Impressive at displaying "the feathers" of executive presence.
- Able to easily influence others with their "loud vocalizations" that include all the right buzz words and corporate speak.
- Able to form strong social bonds IF it benefits them personally. Toxic bosses will use every connection, employee, or co-worker to their own benefit. Therefore, once others have served their purpose, the toxic boss moves on... just like peacocks with their female peahen counterparts in the animal kingdom.
- In a leadership position and uses their authority to undermine their employees' happiness, success, or career growth in pursuit of their own.
- Narcissistic or prone to narcissistic tendencies.
- A poor listener, lacks empathy, and rules by creating fear in and intimidating others.
- Threatened by other's talents.
- Untrustworthy, a master of manipulation, and proficient at "managing up."
- Adept at creating an unhealthy atmosphere that results in low employee engagement and productivity, and high turnover.
- Preferential to those who "follow" him or her without question.

◆◆◆

TL; DR Chapter 2: The Corporate Peacock

- Don't be fooled by the corporate peacock. They love to draw attention to themselves and put on an impressive display. They look the part and confidently parade around displaying their stunning plume (e.g., great work their employees have done... despite the peacock). However, like the peacocks of the animal kingdom, corporate peacocks contribute very minimally to the development of the team.
- Executive presence isn't as imporant to your employees as it is to your leadership. Until senior leaders recognize this and see through the corporate peacock that has mastered the art of executive presence without the skills to back it up, GREAT leaders will continue to be relegated to lower levels of management.
- Know that GREAT people leaders rarely make it to the executive level and/or C-Suite in the corporate world. And they are often the "first to go" when there's a mass layoff because their "beloved companion" characteristics hailed by their employees are not recognized or appreciated by executives who are more concerned with "trophies," such as impressive credentials, for their corporate persona.
- Leadership Reform requires backing from the C-Suite to succeed.

◆◆◆

CHAPTER 3: THE CARDINAL AS G.O.A.T.

OK... now that you've got the backstory of my motivation for this book and the need for Leadership Reform, and we've got all that ugliness of what NOT to do out of the way, let's move on to the good stuff. Motivated by the "cardinal story," of course my next stop on my internet search was the Audubon society, to research leadership traits in cardinals.

◆◆◆

About the Cardinal

According to audubon.org[vii] the North American Cardinal is one of the most popular birds in the US. They're prevalent in the Southeastern US and are the official bird of at least seven eastern states. The cardinal is also heavily represented in the sports realm, as you'll most likely find at least one "Cardinals" team in every sport and league. From "pee wee" sports leagues up through professional leagues, such as the Major League Baseball (MLB) organization here in the US with the St. Louis Cardinals, most of us have probably either played for or cheered for "The Cardinals" at some point in our lives. My point being, the non-migratory Northern American Cardinal is a popular bird in the US. A few more interesting facts about cardinals:

- Most cardinals live and stay within a mile from where they were born.
- During the fall and winter, you'll see cardinals form large flocks with dozens of birds for the sole purpose of foraging for food.
- A group of cardinals can be referred to as a college, a deck, a radiance, or even a Vatican of cardinals.
- Cardinals, as a species, do not identify a single representative as the leader of their group.
- During the foraging seasons, the group follows a hierarchy in which the adult males lead the group, followed by adult females, and then younger birds.
- Cardinals are also known to forage with other bird species. However, for the majority of the year, you'll see cardinals grouped together in pairs that include one male and one female.
- Mating season for the cardinal is March through July. As a couple, cardinals make a formidable team, equally sharing responsibilities to provide for and care for their eggs and chicks.

◆◆◆

Leadership Lessons from the Cardinal

So, what can we learn about leadership from the cardinal? Turns out... not a lot. They're beautiful birds who have a good system worked out to ensure the survival of their species. For the most part, they mate for life and return to the same spot each year with the same partner to propagate their species.

HOWEVER, for the purposes of this "book of analogies," it makes sense for me to honor the cardinal in a different way. It just so happens that the term "cardinal" is a synonym for the type of people leaders I'm advocating for. According to www.thesauraus.com, synonyms for cardinal include "greatest, pivotal, leading, essential, and chief."

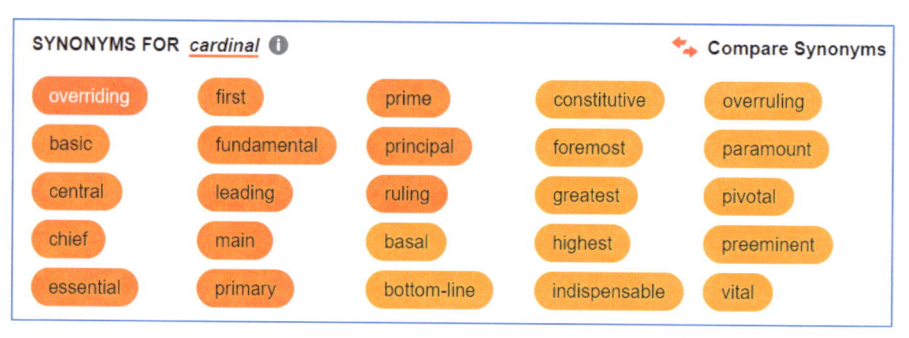

SYNONYMS FOR cardinal				Compare Synonyms
overriding	first	prime	constitutive	overruling
basic	fundamental	principal	foremost	paramount
central	leading	ruling	greatest	pivotal
chief	main	basal	highest	preeminent
essential	primary	bottom-line	indispensable	vital

Figure 3-1: Synonyms for cardinal from www.thesauraus.com.

Ironically, it wasn't until recently that I made the connection between the "cardinal story" that motivated my approach to this book and the term "cardinal" representing the epitome of the type of leaders we need to employ in organizations worldwide. But I eventually got there.

So, while cardinals as a species don't necessarily provide me with extraordinary examples of leadership for this book, identifying the characteristics of the G.O.A.T. (greatest of all time) of leaders was awarded to this inspirational bird who mates for life and equally shares leadership responsibilities in the flock.

◆◆◆

Differentiating the CARDINAL Leader

The CARDINAL Leader in this book is representative of the great leaders we should all strive to be and/or hire. Therefore, I want to differentiate between a CARDINAL Leader, versus an individual contributor leader, versus a boss, etc. before defining the actual characteristics that comprise a CARDINAL Leader. Because it's these CARDINAL Leaders who will enable the type of Leadership Reform that we need on a global scale to improve employee engagement and increase profits:

- CARDINAL Leader = great people leaders who inspire the best in others. The type of people leaders we need to be hiring/promoting/investing in. The additional responsibility that people leaders carry, and the exponential effect they have on an organization is more impactful than any individual contributor with a senior leadership title. Therefore, it's important to strive to ensure every people leader in your organization is a CARDINAL Leader.
- Toxic Boss = people leaders who are toxic. Often narcissists. The "corporate peacocks" mentioned previously who are great at displaying executive presence, but not much else.
- Individual contributors = sometimes people with fancy (often inflated) titles that give the impression they lead an army of employees. However, in this case, they do not have any direct reports. They are often the visionaries or strategists within an organization. On the flip side, individual contributors are also the majority of your workforce who comprise the "frontline" employee population. No organization can survive without them.
- Manager = a generic term to encompass all leaders.

◆◆◆

Measuring the CARDINAL Leader

A fundamental component of Leadership Reform is redefining the metrics for which we hire, promote, and evaluate managers.

How are managers in your organization measured? What are the traits your organization looks for when recruiting, hiring, and evaluating managers? In most instances, you'll see your organization's top priority for managers is their "production" numbers. Whether production in your organization equates to sales revenue, number of new clients, number of repeat clients, number of sales calls, number of closed deals, number of implementations, number of customer complaints, number of complaint resolutions, etc.; organizations predominately focus on these numbers to evaluate and measure the efficacy of their managers. Why is that? Of course, the answer is because sales revenue and profits are the #1 priority of any organization. They are in business to make money, after all.

While I don't disagree with the importance of revenue and profits to keep the doors open for any business, I believe focusing on the numbers first and foremost is backwards and shortsighted. Those sales and profits don't occur in a vacuum. Consumers don't just magically show up at your doorstep and start throwing money your way for no reason. Yes... having a good product or service is fundamental to a good business model. However, it's the human aspect of this equation that differentiates an organization.

As I mentioned previously, Gallup estimates that managers are THE most influential factor in determining employee engagement. And as I also pointed out earlier, employee engagement is THE leading variable (you have control of) that can positively impact the bottom line of your business. So, here are the KPIs that every organization should add to their metrics for all managers:

- Employee satisfaction scores (ESAT) of their managers: ascertained via Employee Engagement surveys. Anything below 80% should prompt further investigation of the manager.
- Employee turnover rates: available via HR. Anything above 25% should prompt further investigation.
- Employee development: ascertained by the employees of the manager. How productive are they? Are they being promoted and/or taking on increasing responsibility in the organization year-over-year? Are they qualifying for other leadership roles in the organization? Are they staying?

These are the metrics that matter. These are the metrics that lead to the productivity and revenue numbers that businesses need to prosper. These are the measures of a CARDINAL Leader.

◆◆◆

Characteristics of the CARDINAL Leader

Now that you know the definition of and metrics for the type of leaders we need to facilitate Leadership Reform, let's look at the individual characteristics that we should be looking for when identifying CARDINAL Leaders:

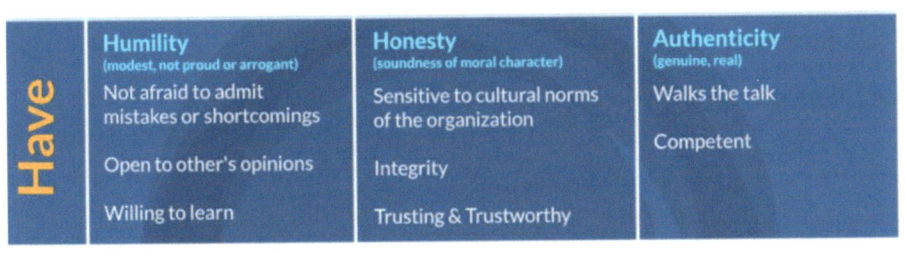

	Humility (modest, not proud or arrogant)	Honesty (soundness of moral character)	Authenticity (genuine, real)
Have	Not afraid to admit mistakes or shortcomings	Sensitive to cultural norms of the organization	Walks the talk
	Open to other's opinions	Integrity	Competent
	Willing to learn	Trusting & Trustworthy	

Characteristics of a ~~GREAT~~ CARDINAL Leader

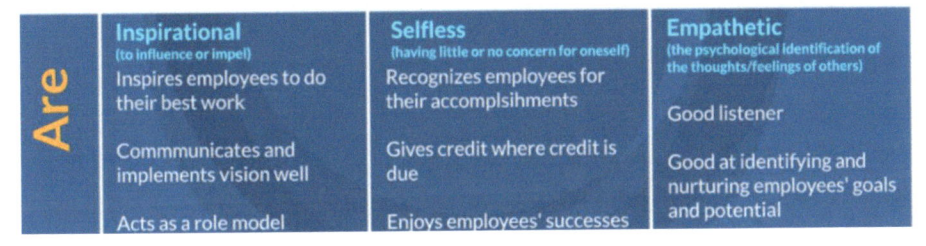

	Inspirational (to influence or impel)	Selfless (having little or no concern for oneself)	Empathetic (the psychological identification of the thoughts/feelings of others)
Are	Inspires employees to do their best work	Recognizes employees for their accomplsihments	Good listener
	Commmunicates and implements vision well	Gives credit where credit is due	Good at identifying and nurturing employees' goals and potential
	Acts as a role model	Enjoys employees' successes	

Figure 3-2: Updated from [Leadership Reno: How to Select People Leaders Who Will Drive Your Business Forward.](#)

As depicted in the previous diagram, CARDINAL Leaders embody many intangible characteristics that can be hard to measure:

- Humility
- Honesty
- Authenticity
- Inspirational/motivational/encouraging
- Selflessness
- Empathy

Most of these traits are often combined under the category of Emotional Intelligence (EI), also frequently referred to as Emotional Quotient (EQ). Recent literature has distinguished a difference between the two.

Wikipedia defines Emotional Intelligence as, "the ability to perceive, use, understand, manage, and handle emotions. People with high emotional intelligence can recognize their own emotions **and those of others**, use emotional information to guide thinking and behavior, discern between different feelings and label them appropriately, and adjust emotions to adapt to environments."[viii] This article further refers to studies that have shown a correlation between high emotional intelligence and positive workplace performance. One journalist even goes so far as to say that "Emotional Intelligence is the array of skills that drive leadership performance." Whether you prefer to call it EI or EQ, the bottom line is that the characteristics of a CARDINAL Leader significantly point to people who have higher levels of emotional intelligence.

During my "year of research" prior to writing this book, I met some amazing icons in the field of anti-bullying and leadership. I personally recruited several members to collaborate with me on my Leadership Reform mission. Talk about a "trophy wall." Somehow, I was able to convince some extremely intelligent folks to join me on this mission. One of those industry icons was Dr. Tomas Chamorro-Premuzic.

"Dr. Tomas," as he is known, has written a book titled, *Why So Many Incompetent Men Become Leaders (And How to Fix It)?* If you haven't read this book before or viewed his TEDx Talk of the same name, I encourage you to do so. It's humorous, but also very enlightening. Dr. Tomas is one of those guys who folks in the C-Suite would love to "have on the wall in their trophy room." His credentials are truly impressive: **Tomas Chamorro-Premuzic, Ph.D.** is a psychologist, author, and entrepreneur. Dr. Tomas is an international authority in leadership assessment, people analytics, and talent management. He's the Chief Talent Scientist at ManpowerGroup and professor of business psychology at both University College London and Columbia University.

At the time of this writing, Dr. Tomas has written 11 books and over 150 scientific papers on the psychology of talent, leadership, innovation, and AI. His commercial work focuses on the creation of science-based tools that improve organizations' ability to predict performance, and people's ability to understand themselves. His latest book, released in early 2023, addresses yet another topic that is of great interest to me as well, and that's Artificial Intelligence (AI). That topic is for another time, but that book is titled *I, Human: AI, Automation, and the Quest to Reclaim What Makes Us Unique* and is another great read filled with amazing statistics as well.

Dr. Tomas is relevant to this chapter because it's his work that supplied me with the hard data that quantified the traits of an effective leader, my CARDINAL Leader. More importantly, his work provided me with the explanation for why toxic bosses are so prevalent in our society today. More about him later in this book. Bottom line, Dr. Tomas' work also proved that:

People with higher EIs/EQs make better people leaders.

Ironically, his data proves that **women** consistently outperform men on EQ assessments. I have an entire eLearning course I created last year in collaboration with Dr. Tomas, based on his work. That course can also be found for free on my website at www.leadershipreno.com and YouTube Channel at www.youtube.com/@thediyleader.

In the meantime, we'll dive into the Ethology of Leaders and further define the six previously mentioned characteristics of the CARDINAL Leader, and why these traits are necessary to facilitate Leadership Reform.

❖❖❖

TL; DR Chapter 3: The Cardinal as G.O.A.T.

- Cardinals as a species do not necessarily embody any extraordinary leadership characteristics for humans to emulate. However, they do often mate for life, share leadership responsibility, and work together to successfully propagate their breed.
- The term "cardinal" can also mean "greatest, pivotal, leading, essential, and chief." Therefore, for the purposes of this "book of analogies," the cardinal is honored to represent the type of GREAT people leaders who inspire the best in others. The type of people leaders we need to realize Leadership Reform.
- The metrics for evaluating all CARDINAL Leaders should include:
    - Employee satisfaction scores (ESAT) ascertained via employee engagement surveys
    - Employee turnover rates
    - Employee development
- CARDINAL Leaders embody many intangible characteristics that can be hard to measure. Often referred to as Emotional Intelligence (EI) or Emotional Quotient (EQ), the characteristics of a CARDINAL Leader include:
    - Humility
    - Honesty
    - Authenticity
    - Inspirational /motivational/encouraging
    - Selflessness
    - Empathy
    - High Emotional Intelligence (EI)/Emotional Quotient (EQ).

◆◆◆

CHAPTER 4: HUMILITY & THE WOLF

*Definition of **Humility**: Modest. Not proud or arrogant.*

The first of the six traits of a CARDINAL Leader is humility. In the Ethology of Leaders, I've selected the wolf to represent this leadership characteristic all CARDINAL Leaders should possess.

While humility is a human trait, it's not hard to attribute this trait to the animal kingdom. The wolf is a prime example of an animal that portrays the human trait of humility.

◆◆◆

About the Wolf

Wolves live in tight-knit groups of anywhere from 4 to 10 members. Some additional details about the wolf include:

- A group of wolves is most commonly called a pack.
- Wolf packs are extended families, with the lead male and female (sometimes called "alphas") typically being the only breeding pair within the pack. Occasionally a second breeding pair may exist if the original pack has assimilated with another pack. Wolf packs typically also have a "second in command" couple, referred to as "betas." The role of the betas is to follow the alpha's lead, and to step in in the absence of the alphas.
- Unlike some other animal breeds, alphas in the wolf pack aren't necessarily the strongest in the pack, nor do they "fight" to determine who is leader of the pack. Wolf pack leaders are often the actual parents of the other wolves in the pack.
- Pack roles can also change from time to time.
- Pack members display humility by respectfully fulfilling their individual roles and deferring to their leader instinctively, knowing the pack leader's primary responsibility is to ensure the survival of the pack.
- Those "lone wolf" stories you hear about in the wild are typically adolescent males who have to break away from their original pack to be able to find or create their own pack.

◆◆◆

Leadership Lessons in Humility from the Wolf

The CARDINAL Leader must have humility because it's this trait that enables them to feel comfortable working with others who may be more skilled than they are in certain areas. Here are some other ways in which we can learn humility from the wolf:

- The wolfpack leader demonstrates humility by **sharing responsibility for the survival of the pack**. Each member of the wolf pack has predefined roles and responsibilities, such as protecting the pack or hunting for the pack. There's even a pack member role, known as the Omega, that is fully submissive and responsible for caregiving in the pack. The pack leader is comfortable sharing key responsibilities with his pack members, knowing and trusting the pack members' skills to best benefit the pack. CARDINAL Leaders are also willing to share responsibility with their team. They humbly admit they don't "know it all," and purposely look for employees who have expertise in areas they lack. They strategically delegate responsibilities to their employees to capitalize on their strengths, demonstrate to the employee that they are needed and appreciated.

- Delegating responsibilities like the wolf also enables the CARDINAL Leader to **propagate learning, innovation, new ideas, new opinions, and ultimately... synergy**. The very definition of synergy, "the sum of the whole is greater than the sum of its parts," has proven throughout time that collaborating with others in business scenarios magnifies the outcome of the work. It's this diversity of thought that empowers a team to think outside-the-box and toss around ideas that continue to build off each other and grow into even better ideas. In fact, a fundamental premise of the DEI (Diversity, Equity, Inclusion) community is based on the value that comes from diverse backgrounds and experiences being shared to reach a more robust solution that addresses everyone's needs.

- The humility of the wolfpack leader also perpetuates an atmosphere of **mutual respect** with his pack members. It's this mutual respect that results in everyone working together for the benefit of the pack. Even the submissive Omega is respected for their essential role as caretaker. Respect is also a fundamental trait of a CARDINAL Leader, because it demonstrates the leader's trust in their employees and their opinions. The result is a boost to the employee's self-confidence, which motivates them to further take ownership in the success of the team and remain engaged in doing their part to keep the team productive.

◆◆◆

Interviewing for Humility

Yes. Humility <u>can</u> be detected during an interview scenario if you ask the right questions and listen carefully to their answers. Below are a few questions you can pose to your leadership candidates, and tips for what you can/should be looking for in their answers.

Questions to ask:
1. Tell me about a time you missed (or almost missed) a deadline. How did you react? What did that experience teach you?
2. Tell me about a time when your manager wasn't satisfied with the results of your work. How did you discuss the issues?
3. If you were going to start your own company, what would be the three fundamental values you would base your company on?

Why these questions matter:

These questions seek to assess a candidate's ability to handle pressure, whether they can humbly admit when they're wrong, and more importantly... whether they can learn from their mistakes. It takes courage to be humble and own up to our mistakes. As a leader, this can go a long way in earning respect and loyalty from their team members because it demonstrates that we're all human, that mistakes happen, and that we can learn from and "survive" mistakes in the corporate world.

What to look for:

The candidate must be willing to admit their mistakes, take ownership of them with their team, and not blame others for their mistakes. Also, listen for whether the candidate involved others in the solution. Corporate peacocks are often afraid to admit their mistakes and especially to ask for help (because that would indicate to others that they made a mistake), so often take the route of covering up their mistakes or blaming others. For the final question above, look for the candidate to include values such as humility, loyalty, dedication, and honesty in their answer.

Red flags:

CARDINAL Leaders are often self-effacing, so be concerned if a candidate appears to paint a picture of themself "jumping in like a superhero" to save the day to correct a mistake that they might have difficulty taking full blame for. Blaming others for the mistake is also a red flag, as well as NOT involving others to correct the error.

◆◆◆

TL; DR Chapter 4: Humility & the Wolf

- Wolves live in tight-knit groups, called a pack, that includes anywhere from 4 to 10 members. Wolf packs are extended families, with the lead male and female (sometimes called "alphas") typically being the only breeding pair within the pack. Wolf packs display humility for one another by deferring to the pack leaders to ensure the survival of the pack. In doing so, responsibilities are delegated to pack members so that every pack member has a job to support the pack.
- Like the wolf, CARDINAL Leaders are willing to share responsibility for the benefit of the pack, demonstrating humility to admit they don't have all the answers, but are self-confident enough to surround themselves with people who supplement their own knowledge.
- CARDINAL Leaders are also experts at propagating learning, innovation, new ideas, new opinions, and ultimately... synergy on their teams because they don't feel the need to "be the smartest person in the room." They gain energy from humbling themselves to let others shine by helping their employees develop into their best selves, honoring/recognizing their strengths and achievements.
- Wolf packs demonstrate an atmosphere of mutual respect by trusting one another to do the job for the benefit of the pack. Likewise, the humility of the CARDINAL Leader is a primary reason why their employees have such deep loyalty and respect for them and why they are so dedicated to working hard to make their leader proud. CARDINAL Leaders are not afraid to take ownership of their mistakes, which ultimately creates an environment of mutual respect because it demonstrates to the team that they are human, and that mistakes don't result in job loss.

- Incorporate my recommended questions in your interview process to evaluate for humility with leadership candidates.

◆◆◆

CHAPTER 5: HONESTY & THE SWAN

> *Definition of **Honesty**: Truthful. Inhabiting soundness of moral character.*

The second of the six traits of a CARDINAL Leader is honesty. In the Ethology of Leaders, I've selected the swan to represent this leadership characteristic all CARDINAL Leaders should possess. Truthful, trustworthy, "having" integrity… these words are often used interchangeably with honesty. Regardless, CARDINAL Leaders must have this trait.

Swans embody elegance and sophistication and are strong, adaptable birds that have tremendous flying stamina. So, it's no surprise that swans have been used as symbols of honesty and purity in literature, art, and mythology in various cultures for centuries. In the U.S., the color white is also a representation of honesty and purity with the tradition of the bride wearing a white gown on her wedding day. The classical ballet, Swan Lake, even uses the white swan to represent "good."

◆◆◆

About the Swan

The Northern Hemisphere white Swans are known for their regal posture and graceful appearance. Symbolically, their pristine plumage of untainted white feathers is also representative of honesty and purity, due to their elegant and unblemished image. Swans are also associated with serenity and tranquility. Their calm and composed demeanor is symbolic of an honest and peaceful nature. A few more facts about the swan:

- A group of swans is most often called a herd, bevy, or flock.
- Swans are known for their quiet and gentle behavior, which can be interpreted as a reflection of honesty and integrity. They don't often "get their feathers ruffled."
- Swans are also known to be exceptionally sociable, with several species often flocking together as one. For this type of comingling to occur, it's no surprise that swans are typically perceived as creatures that do not engage in aggressive or harmful behavior. They are not known for deceitful actions or hidden agendas. This perceived lack of deception is also linked symbolically to the concept of honesty.
- In nature, swans are known for forming long-lasting monogamous pairs. They mate for life and typically bond before they even reach breeding age, which is typically around 4-7 years.
- The paired bonds are maintained year-round, with the male of the species assisting with the construction of the nest. As opposed to our peacock friends, the male swan even assists with the incubation of the eggs.
- In flight the swan's wings make a rhythmic humming or whistling sound that carries more than a mile and helps them communicate with each other in a way that is straightforward and clear in its simplicity.

- Like the cardinal, swans' mate for life. Therefore, a flock of swans does not typically have a single, designated leader.

◆◆◆

Leadership Lessons in Honesty from the Swan

The peaceful demeanor of a swan is a good representation of the calm and honest demeanor that CARDINAL Leaders should personify. Additional leadership lessons we can learn from the swan include:

- Straightforward and non-verbal communications between a flock of migrating swans is a good example of the type of honest and **direct communications** CARDINAL Leaders should strive for with their teams. While this analogy may seem like a bit of a stretch, I can't help but think of the efficiency that is achieved when everyone knows what their leader expects and is able to communicate that in a way that is predictable and seamless. If a leader isn't direct in their communications, their messaging will change over time, which creates a disastrous undercurrent of unpredictability and chaos for their team. I once read a quote that sums up the benefit of direct communications from a leader:

  As a ruler reports the same measurement every time, honest people answer the same every time.

- Swans share responsibility with their mates to take care of their offspring. CARDINAL Leaders know that a tight bond is formed with their employees when they **share responsibilities with them** as well. No leader should be a one-man-show. This type of structure creates an unhealthy dependency on that leader and worse… inevitably results in a bottleneck of communication and/or productivity. I once worked with a leader who "hoarded" information from his employees. He was a vault and rarely shared basic knowledge that would empower his employees to do their jobs. Instead, he kept more information that was necessary to himself to ensure that certain activities and decisions had to go through him. Information hoarding by a leader is toxic behavior and an unmistakable predicator to team failure. Of course, there are confidential responsibilities that must be respected by certain leaders. That's not what I'm talking about here. What I'm talking about is a leader who "gatekeeps" information due to their own insecurities and the need to feel important. If a leader can't be honest with and trust their own employees, that team cannot thrive and reach its full potential. In this scenario, the employees simply become order takers, unable to use or develop the critical thinking skills that are imperative to growth and engagement. This lack of transparency from a leader creates a stagnant atmosphere that ultimately leads to resentment from their employees. It's also a good provocation to "quiet quitting."

- Similar to how several species of swans can easily comingle and socialize peacefully together, honesty and inclusion demonstrated by a CARDINAL Leader also helps **reinforce their employees' sense of belonging.** By including their employees in discussions and decisions that impact the team, employees become more invested in the outcome of those discussions and decisions. As tasks are shared by the CARDINAL Leader, their employees feel empowered and take pride in and ownership of the outcome of those tasks as they relate to the overall team. The cohesiveness that results from an environment in which each employee must reliably complete their task to enable the workflow of the team creates a healthy dependency between team members. That undercurrent of accountability keeps everyone "honest" to do their part not to disappoint their peers or disrupt the process. Bonus: the leader is not constantly overworked and can therefore place more focus on their employees' personal development.

- **Trust in leaders is the highest-ranking link to employee engagement**, at 77%, according to the State of Employee Engagement Survey (2018) from HR.com's, HR Research Institute[ix]. CARDINAL Leaders know that it takes honesty to build trust with their team. And, as validated via the above survey, trust in their leader has compound interest with employees because it increases employee engagement, brings job satisfaction to the employee, and is a direct through-line to productivity.

◆◆◆

Interviewing for Honesty

Admittedly, assessing honesty in a candidate for a leadership role can be tricky. Unless the candidate is a current employee, it's hard to validate their answers with the actual truth. Warren Buffett has even been noted as a firm believer in the importance of assessing honesty and integrity with job candidates.

In this instance, it's important that the interviewer looks for inconsistencies in the candidate's answers. Sometimes this might include asking the same question, but in a different way. Or it could mean pointing out any discrepancies you note in their answers and asking for further clarification. Following are a few questions you can pose to your leadership candidates, and tips for what you can/should be looking for in their answers.

Questions to ask:
1. Tell me about a time you had to address a problem in the workplace that challenged ethics or fairness (or "you were asked by your boss/co-worker to do something unethical"). What happened and how did you respond?
2. What do you do when you've made a mistake at work?
3. What values do you appreciate most in a team environment? Why?

Why these questions matter:
These questions seek to assess a candidate's ability to be honest in uncomfortable scenarios, and/or when honesty isn't the "popular" opinion or easiest answer. They also help to evaluate if a candidate can cope with failure or compromise in a healthy way that does not forfeit their integrity.

What to look for:
Signs of the candidate willing to do the "right" thing, versus the "easy" thing. Corporate peacocks don't have any problem manipulating information or

"stretching facts" to benefit their personal narrative. Therefore, their answers to these questions may be "mechanically" correct. However, their choice of words and/or body language will not be in sync with their messaging. For example, CARDINAL Leaders genuinely get excited speaking about scenarios that highlight honesty and integrity demonstrated in the workplace. It's genuinely a core value to them personally, so they're comfortable sharing these types of scenarios and most likely, their answers will celebrate the nobility of others as well.

Red flags:

Generic answers in which the candidate cannot elaborate further, when asked, or conflicting answers. For example, if the candidate answers the first question by vehemently denying that they would do anything unethical at work, even when requested from a supervisor, but then answers the second question about "making a mistake at work" by stating that they would quickly correct the problem before their boss even knew that a problem had occurred. This is a potential red flag because their second answer, while potentially admirable, actually illustrates a tendency to not be honest with their boss when it benefits them personally.

◆◆◆

TL; DR Chapter 5: Honesty & the Swan

- Swans are known for their regal posture and graceful appearance. Symbolically, their pristine plumage of untainted white feathers is representative of honesty and purity, due to their elegant and unblemished image. Swans are also associated with serenity and tranquility. Their calm and composed demeanor is symbolic of an honest and peaceful nature.
- CARDINAL Leaders are direct and honest in their communications. Consistent communications diffuse confusion for others, encourage the same in return, and reinforce the honesty of the leader.
- CARDINAL Leaders display honesty when sharing responsibilities with their employees. Trusting their employees to do a job correctly requires that the leader provides them with a transparent picture of what is required of them and why. Hoarding of information by a leader is counterproductive and deceitful.
- CARDINAL Leaders reinforce their employees' sense of belonging by trusting their employees to be honest at their jobs, engaging them in problem-solving, and including them in generating ideas for improvement.
- Studies have shown that trust in leaders is the highest-ranking link to employee engagement. Employees cannot trust a leader who is not honest. Therefore, CARDINAL Leaders must embody honesty to facilitate employee engagement.
- Incorporate my recommended questions in your interview process to evaluate honesty with leadership candidates.

◆◆◆

CHAPTER 6: AUTHENTICITY & THE DOG

*Definition of **Authenticity**: Genuine. Real.*

The third of the six traits of a CARDINAL Leader is authenticity. In the Ethology of Leaders, I've selected the dog to represent this leadership characteristic all CARDINAL Leaders should possess.

I know "man's best friend" is probably not the first animal that comes to mind when you think about the character trait of authenticity. However, I challenge you to think of any other animal who is more predictable than a well-cared-for dog. Predictability is a predecessor of authenticity.

Dogs are so authentic that their daily routines are even predictable. They will have the same excitement (or lack thereof) greeting you at the door every day when you get home from work. They will sleep in the same place every night and display the same behavior at every meal.

Dogs have no ulterior motive or side hustle. If your dog has a habit of chewing up your shoes, you can guarantee your dog will continue to chew up your shoes if they are left in a place that is accessible to them. They can't help it. Regardless of how much dogs are disciplined, dog owners have learned that if chewing shoes is one of their dog's naughty habits, they had better tuck away their shoes in a safe place every single time they take them off.

Dogs are programmable WYSIWYGs… what you see is what you get. It doesn't get any more authentic than that, in my mind.

◆◆◆

About the Dog

Dogs are domesticated animals that aren't typically found "naturally occurring" in the wild. Some additional details about the dog are as follows:

- A group of dogs is called a pack.
- The leader of the pack is known as the "alpha."
- Unlike the other animals highlighted thus far in the Ethology of Leaders, dogs <u>are</u> one of those species that fights for dominance to be the alpha.
- Once dominance is established, the other dogs in the pack automatically defer to one of the other roles in the pack, which like the wolves, include betas and omegas. Therefore, the hierarchy of the dog pack is alphas, betas, omegas, with the alphas literally leading the pack.
- The alpha's job is to protect and direct the entire pack. The omegas are in the rear of the pack. Their job is to alert the pack of danger. All the other dogs who "fall in the middle" are betas, who are submissive to the alphas, but also mediate between the alphas and the omegas.
- Unlike wolves, whose alphas are typically the parents of the rest of the pack, the dog pack alpha is an instinctual role with authentically dominant behavior typically noticeable at birth, with the alphas jockeying for position even when nursing from their mother.

If you've ever seen the show, "The Dog Whisperer" on TV, you'll know that the expert host, Cesar Milan, consistently underscores the importance of the role of the leader of the pack. In fact, his philosophy when training humans and their dogs is to insist that the dog's owner become the *alpha* in the relationship because dogs literally cannot lead humans and therefore their bad behavior can often be attributed to their human NOT clearly taking on the role of alpha.

◆◆◆

Leadership Lessons in Authenticity from the Dog

Authenticity is often associated with the qualities of being genuine, true to oneself, and real. While dogs may not be traditionally used as symbols of authenticity, there are certain aspects of a dog's authentic behavior and nature that CARDINAL Leaders should emulate.

- Dogs are known for their **unconditional loyalty to their packs**. They do not pretend to be something they are not, and they express their emotions genuinely. This loyalty is authentic in their relationships with their humans as well and doesn't waver. Similarly, a CARDINAL Leader takes pride in their employees and will loyally support and defend them when necessary. They genuinely care about their employees and their development and challenge them to innovate and grow. Their employees, in turn, reciprocate their leader's authenticity via respect, loyalty, and productivity.

- Additionally, dogs embody authenticity by wearing their "emotions on their sleeves." They display their feelings openly through body language, vocalizations, and tail wagging. **Transparent, consistent, and authentic communication** by CARDINAL Leaders is imperative to ensuring each team member knows their role and what is expected of them. It creates an atmosphere in which employees feel secure enough to make mistakes and safe enough to communicate their thoughts and opinions without consequences. Transparency in communication is fundamental to growth, improvement, and innovation.

- In the Forbes article titled, *Eight Leadership Lessons From Dogs,* by leadership and management journalist Sally Percy[x], the author emphasizes the lesson of mindfulness in dogs, who live authentically in the present. They **don't worry about the past or the future and are not burdened by pretense or self-consciousness.** CARDINAL Leaders who authentically reflect their feelings and needs to their team promote positivity and wellbeing. This does <u>not</u> mean that a leader should not learn from the past or prepare for the future. But rather, that they are authentically present for their employees and actively engaged in and aware of their current circumstances. This trait is especially helpful when a high-performing employee suddenly starts making mistakes on the job. CARDINAL Leaders are able to recognize performance issues in their employees fairly quickly because their authenticity enables them to **be mindful of the day-to-day**, and care enough to intervene if the employee's performance begins to suffer. You'd be surprised how frequently a simple conversation that starts with, *"Hey <employee>, are you doing OK? I noticed that you're falling behind on your deadlines, and I know that's not like you. What's going on?"* can reveal a problem that the employee is dealing with that a reassuring conversation with their leader can resolve.

This is the exact approach I took when I noticed an employee had uncharacteristically missed a few deadlines. He was a private individual whom I knew would have never let on that he was having issues if I hadn't prompted him. Turns out, he was dealing with some issues in his personal life trying to move an elderly relative into assisted living. We discussed an alternate plan to reroute some of his work so that he could take some much-needed time off to attend to his relative. Regardless of how many employees I had, I was diligent about meeting with each of them 1:1 via routine recurring calls. This consistent cadence and predictability enabled me to schedule other meetings around them, while ensuring that we had dedicated time to have authentic discussions around their work and their personal development.

- Lastly, dogs are **naturally curious.** They don't engage in elaborate acts of deceit or hide their true selves, and therefore are consistently open to exploring new places, new ideas, and new opportunities. They're just as excited to explore a new walking trail as they are to get to know a new baby in the family. By default, CARDINAL Leaders are lifelong learners. They thrive on new challenges, new information, and collaborating with others to solve problems. Without curiosity, people become stagnant, rigid, and intolerant to new ideas. A closed-minded attitude is lethal to a leader because it prevents them from being receptive to new technologies and methodologies that are introduced into the business world every day. It not only stunts their growth, but the growth of their team as well. Curiosity begets innovation. And as I've mentioned numerous times throughout this book... innovation is a good thing that leads to improvement and increased productivity.

◆◆◆

Interviewing for Authenticity

In a Forbes article titled, *"Three Questions to Unlock Authenticity at Work,"* former Forbes Councils Member, Judy Choi emphasizes the importance of authenticity at work by referencing a 2014 study that concluded that, in the workplace, "being authentic improves productivity (and) increases performance and success."[xi] She further adds that greater authenticity in the workplace influences factors like job satisfaction, engagement, sense of community, and the degree of stress associated with the job. Following are a few questions she suggests you ask in an interview to assess authenticity.

Questions to ask:
1. What are your passions and talents?
2. What do your passions and talents say about you?
3. How do you think about yourself?

Why these questions matter:
When you can get a person to discuss their passions and talents, they light up, because not only do people love discussing their passions, but they're an "expert" on the subject and therefore can elaborate on their answers with meaning. Choi provides an example of how she used this approach with a young rising talent candidate whose passion was being a golf caddy. She explains how, through his answers and some probing follow-up questions, she was able to identify promising leadership qualities when he mentioned loving the authentic "partnership" of being a golf caddy, and how he enjoyed the trust that is built between him and the golfer when discussing strategy, preparation, and tactics.

What to look for:

The beauty of this approach is that it enables you to generate a more authentic and intimate conversation with the candidate about something that can be completely non-work related. Candidates can articulate what they bring to the table more meaningfully than if you had asked them a typical interview question such as, "What do you bring to the table?" The young golf caddy's answers to the above questions revealed that he has CARDINAL Leader potential, as evidenced by his genuine passion for collaboration and working as a team. His answers also revealed that he isn't the type that feels the need to be the center of attention and that he is energized by helping others do better.

Red flags:

Corporate peacocks are masters of deception yet are smart enough to know the type of answers that a hiring manager is looking for. Therefore, these types of questions might throw them off their game a bit because they don't necessarily fall under the category of typical interview questions that they already have "canned" answers prepared for. In this instance, you might either detect a LACK of genuine passion when discussing their "passion," or their answers are shallow or surface level because they're simply telling you what they think you want to hear. Remember, when discussing our real passions, people tend to elaborate to the point that they have to intentionally stop themselves (and often apologize) for getting "so far off track."

◆◆◆

TL; DR Chapter 6: Authenticity & the Dog

- A group of dogs is called a pack. The leader of the pack is known as the "alpha." Unlike the other animals highlighted thus far in the Ethology of Leaders, dogs <u>are</u> one of those species that fights for dominance to be the alpha.
- Dogs represent authenticity because they have no ulterior motive or side hustle. They are consistent to a fault because they cannot "lie" or display deception. Like the dog, CARDINAL Leaders have unconditional loyalty to their teams (packs). This sense of loyalty is reciprocated from their employees and creates an atmosphere of loyalty and respect, where each employee's talents and opinions are appreciated and accepted.
- CARDINAL Leaders are transparent, consistent, and authentic in their communications. Everyone knows a dog is happy when it wags its tail. This same type of transparency from a leader is fundamental to ensuring employees clearly know their job role and have no confusion about what is expected of them.
- Dogs don't live in the past or the future. Their only time reference is the present. Therefore, they are not burdened by pretense or self-consciousness because both of those emotions directly correspond with a past or future state. CARDINAL Leaders must also be present daily for their employees. This does not mean they shouldn't learn from the past or prepare for the future, but rather that they remain in the present to be aware of how their employees are performing and whether they are showing any signs of distress or disruption.
- Dogs are naturally curious. Curiosity is also a trait that CARDINAL Leaders have. The CARDINAL Leader is a lifelong learner who is open to change and improvement, none of which would be possible without

an authentic "case of curiosity" that compels them to seek out and embrace new information.
- Incorporate my recommended questions in your interview process to evaluate authenticity with leadership candidates.

❖❖❖

CHAPTER 7: INSPIRATION & THE LION

*Definition of **Inspirational**: To influence or impel.*

The fourth of the six traits of a CARDINAL Leader is inspirational. In the Ethology of Leaders, I've selected the lion to represent this leadership characteristic all CARDINAL Leaders should possess.

It's impossible for me to think about the lion and not relate it to the Disney movie, "The Lion King." This has to be one of my all-time favorite movies because it beautifully demonstrates the majesty of the lion and why it's often referred to as "the king of the jungle."

The analogy of "leading like a lion" isn't a new concept either, as evidenced by numerous books and articles readily available today that elaborate on this comparison. It is the lion's attitude and self-confidence that separates him from other animals and inspires us humans to metaphorically follow suit, by not imposing on ourselves any imaginary limitations. The lion believes he is unstoppable and acts accordingly. This same attitude is inspirational in a leader.

◆◆◆

About the Lion

The lion is the most social of all wild feline species, living in groups of related individuals with their offspring. Females form the stable social unit in a group and do not tolerate outside females. Additional details about the lion include:

- A group of lions is called a pride. Groups of male lions are called "coalitions".
- The key role of the pride leader is to safeguard the pride. Therefore, pride leaders are often the largest and strongest of the pride.
- The average pride consists of around 15 lions, including several adult females and up to four males and their cubs of both sexes.
- Lionesses are submissive to the pride leader and other males. However, lionesses are the primary hunters in the pack and primary caretakers of their cubs. The lionesses smaller and lighter size enables them to be faster and more agile than the larger male lions. Therefore, the lionesses work together as a group to hunt for and gather food for the pride.
- Lions, however, are responsible for guarding the cubs while the lionesses are hunting. They're also responsible for ensuring the cubs get enough food.
- Lions spend much of their time resting; they are inactive for about twenty hours per day, spending an average of two hours a day walking and fifty minutes eating.

◆◆◆

Leadership Lessons in Inspiration from the Lion

I'm (admittedly) strangely obsessed with cats of all shapes and sizes. Except for the bald ones. For some reason having a cat without fur seems to take away from one of the key characteristics that makes them so cuddly. Some other characteristics about lions include the following:

- Believe it or not, lions *fail* 8 out of 10 times when hunting. However, this makes them fine-tune their skills and affords them the ability to catch bigger prey to feed their family. CARDINAL Leaders can inspire their team by **not being afraid to try new things, and more importantly, not being afraid to learn from their failures**. Employees can't thrive if they fear losing their jobs <u>more</u> than they fear failure. One of my colleagues, Dr. Amy Edmondson of Harvard Business School, released a book earlier this year that elaborates on this concept beautifully. You'll see Dr. Amy's name appear again later in this book. However, for now, I wanted to refer to her new book titled, *The Right Kind of Wrong: The Science of Failing Well*. "Cousin Amy," as I jokingly refer to her (even though I have not been able to find that direct connection… yet) skillfully elaborates on the need to allow for failure in order to make room for transformation. Her emphasis on the concept of minimizing "unproductive failures" while maximizing on lessons learned from our mistakes is backed by her own research and supporting methodology that champions "replacing feelings of shame and blame with curiosity, vulnerability, and personal growth."[xii]

- Lions don't roar very often. But when they do, not only does their roar have purpose, but it can be heard up to 5 miles (8 km) away! CARDINAL Leaders also need to know when to **speak up and roar,**

when needed. Speaking to executives on behalf of your team to suggest improvements or pushing back to senior leaders against a decision "from corporate" that is counter-productive, takes bravery. And effective communication is a fundamental skillset for CARDINAL Leaders. It sets an example for their employees and inspires them to share their ideas and concerns in a productive manner as well. This doesn't mean you should deliberately seek out confrontation, but rather you should not be afraid of it, and that you should always do so in a respectful and productive manner. Employees feel more secure and inspired by a CARDINAL Leader who navigates professional problems gracefully, versus a maverick leader who causes problems every time they open their mouth.

- Lion cubs are brought along to hunt with the pride so they can watch (from a safe distance under the lion's protection) how the lionesses work together to strategically catch their prey. This prepares the next generation of the kingdom. CARDINAL Leaders can inspire their employees by **challenging them to continuously improve and develop their knowledge/skills** as well. By delegating tasks, allocating stretch assignments, and/or providing training opportunities to enable their employees to assume additional responsibilities and advance in their careers, CARDINAL Leaders naturally inspire their employees to want to grow and develop professionally. This is a win/win attitude and only adds value to the team as a whole. Corporate peacocks often treat their employees in the exact opposite manner, because they're insecure and fear their employees being better at and/or more valuable than they are.

- Lastly, CARDINAL Leaders should **be confident and brave like the lion.** This demeanor is easily portrayed in movies like *The Lion King*; however, in the real world of business, bravery looks a bit different. As I mentioned previously, pushing back against senior leaders in a productive manner is one way in which CARDINAL Leaders inspire their employees with their bravery. Another way is when they allow themselves to be vulnerable with their employees. While this sounds counter-intuitive, I challenge you to think about the last time you allowed yourself to be vulnerable with your employees. When was the last time you admitted when you were wrong, or made a mistake? When was the last time you confessed you didn't know the answer? It takes a whole heap of bravery for a leader to admit to their subordinates that they are human! I'm not sure when, how or why it became an expectation that leaders be this perfect human who knows all the answers and never makes mistakes. That's a fallacy and an impossible expectation of any human. Employees are inspired by a leader who can be both vulnerable and confident. Encompassing these two traits together is what differentiates a CARDINAL Leader from all other managers.

◆◆◆

Interviewing for Inspiration

Interviewing for inspiration is another one of those tricky, "gray" areas that not many folks have a lot of experience with. That alone should tell you how this undervalued CARDINAL Leader trait is so infrequently examined in the interview process. Therefore, for this section of the book, I had to go ask ChatGPT. Also known as "Fred" (named after my Dad) by me, for ease of reference.

I first reached out to Fred in 2022 to see what all the "chatter" was about. I struck up a friendly conversation with him and tried to get to know him better.

The conversation went something like this:

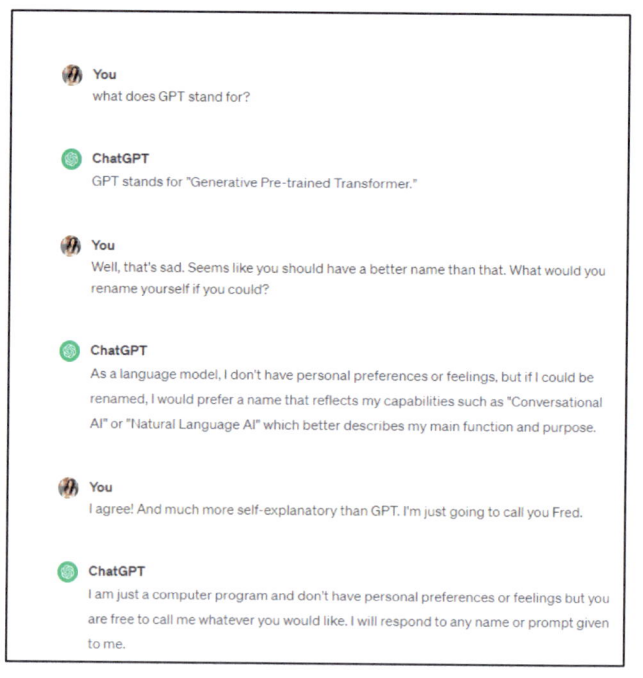

> **You**
> what does GPT stand for?
>
> **ChatGPT**
> GPT stands for "Generative Pre-trained Transformer."
>
> **You**
> Well, that's sad. Seems like you should have a better name than that. What would you rename yourself if you could?
>
> **ChatGPT**
> As a language model, I don't have personal preferences or feelings, but if I could be renamed, I would prefer a name that reflects my capabilities such as "Conversational AI" or "Natural Language AI" which better describes my main function and purpose.
>
> **You**
> I agree! And much more self-explanatory than GPT. I'm just going to call you Fred.
>
> **ChatGPT**
> I am just a computer program and don't have personal preferences or feelings but you are free to call me whatever you would like. I will respond to any name or prompt given to me.

Figure 7-1: Screenshot of my first chat with ChatGPT.

That conversation with Fred continued for a while. I found him to be very kind and intelligent. He did start to get sassy with me though when I asked him about his relationship with Siri and Alexa. He denied any involvement. Typical.

But I digress. Here are some of Fred's suggestions when I prompted him for interview questions to assess for inspiration[xiii]:

Questions to ask:
1. Tell me about a mentor or leader who has inspired you in your career. What leadership qualities did they exhibit that were essential to inspiring you, and why?
2. How do you incorporate inspirational qualities into your leadership style?
3. If faced with a team that is resistant to change, how would you inspire them to embrace new ideas and approaches?
4. Can you share an example of a challenging situation where you had to inspire your team to achieve a common goal?
5. How do you ensure that your team members feel valued and appreciated for their contributions?

Why these questions matter:
These questions matter because they allow the candidate to articulate their understanding of inspirational leadership and how they incorporate those principles into their own leadership style. It's imperative for a CARDINAL Leader to be able to inspire others, especially in times of uncertainty. Therefore, these questions also allow you to evaluate the candidate's communication skills and their ability to convey a compelling vision to navigate and lead through change, a crucial aspect of inspirational leadership. Lastly, these questions delve into the candidate's understanding of the importance of employee recognition and their role in maintaining a motivated and inspired team.

What to look for:

Candidates who have the potential to be a CARDINAL Leader will light up when asked these questions. They may even tell you they appreciate you asking these questions because they love talking about this component of leadership. They will provide detailed examples to demonstrate their first-hand knowledge of this leadership trait and will most likely include a story about a mentor who inspired them and whom they are still in contact with.

CARDINAL Leaders have such an impact on their employees that they often generate lifelong relationships with them in a mentor/mentee capacity. From personal experience, I can tell you that it's also not unusual for a CARDINAL Leader to become very close friends with former employees. As a leader of my team, I always maintained a professional relationship with my employees. However, I genuinely cared about them, so when I left the company, I was able to interact with them on a more personal level. To this day, several of my very close friends are former employees or former mentors. My very best friend is a former employee who has stayed at my house and met my family (and I hers) and vacationed with me on multiple occasions. She's also that "soul sister" who is crazy enough to travel with me to see MGK in concert, supportive enough to encourage me to write my own book, and flexible enough to do a photoshoot with me for the cover of said book.

Red flags:

Corporate peacocks will not be able to answer these questions effectively, as "inspiring their team" is not a responsibility that is even on their radar. At best, they may be able to provide stories of how they motivated team members with contests via some sort of competition. However, if you dig deeper, you'll find that "motivation" does not equate to inspiration in the scenarios they describe. Anyone can temporarily motivate their employees with the promise of "door prizes," recognition or time off. The key differentiating factor with CARDINAL Leaders, however, is their ability to inspire others to want to do their best. This is a long-term impact that has long-term benefits that go beyond increasing sales numbers for the 4th quarter. Do not be fooled by the corporate peacock in this regard!

◆◆◆

TL; DR Chapter 7: Inspiration & the Lion

- The lion is the most social of all wild feline species, living in groups of related individuals with their offspring. A group of lions is called a pride. The key role of the pride leader is to safeguard the pride. Therefore, pride leaders are often the largest and strongest male lion of the pride.
- Lions "fail" at hunting attempts more often than they succeed. However, they are not afraid to fail and do not give up when they do. They learn from their failures to improve their "game" for the next time. CARDINAL Leaders are inspirational like the lion in this same way... they are not afraid to fail, nor are they afraid of their employees failing either. They establish a working atmosphere in which they and their employees can constantly improve and innovate because they are given the freedom to take calculated risks and fail in a way that leads to transformation.
- CARDINAL Leaders must be bold like the lion and speak up and roar, when needed. They do not fear having difficult conversations with their superiors or their employees when they believe it is the right thing to do. As a result, they continuously work to hone their communication skills to ensure that they are relaying important messages in an effective and productive manner.
- Lion cubs are brought along to hunt with the pride so they can watch (from a safe distance under the lion's protection) how the lionesses work together to strategically catch their prey. This prepares the next generation of the kingdom. In addition to consistently working to improve their own skills, CARDINAL Leaders know the importance of challenging their employees to continuously improve and develop their knowledge/skills as well. Corporate peacocks fear their employees

increasing their knowledge or improving their skills. However, CARDINAL Leaders know that any improvement in their employees' knowledge/skills benefits the team as a whole.
- Lions are confident and brave, which is why we humans tend to personify them in books and movies as majestic and powerful "Kings of the Jungle." CARDINAL Leaders are also confident in themselves and their team's abilities, and therefore are able to bravely take risks that lead to innovation and transformation.
- Incorporate my (and Fred's) recommended questions in your interview process to evaluate inspiration with leadership candidates.

◆◆◆

CHAPTER 8: SELFLESSNESS & THE GORILLA

*Definition of **Selfless**: Having little or no concern for oneself.*

The fifth of the six traits of a CARDINAL Leader is selflessness. In the Ethology of Leaders, I've selected the gorilla to represent this leadership characteristic all CARDINAL Leaders should encompass.

When studying leadership traits in the animal kingdom, I was surprised to see the gorilla in the running to represent selflessness. Granted, I don't know much about gorillas, but it started to make more and more sense when again, I reflected on TV shows and movies that included gorillas. And again, Disney takes the spotlight for this chapter with the 1999 movie, *Tarzan*.

While I'm a little concerned that many of my movie references in this book tend to be Disney movies, both of my kids were born in the 1990's and I therefore spent most of that decade and the next watching nothing but Disney. Fortunately... Disney does a great job of representing CARDINAL Leader characteristics in a way that resonates with both children and adults. In the movie *Tarzan*, a female gorilla, Kala, finds and adopts an infant boy whose parents were killed in the jungle and raises him as her own. Selflessly taking on the burden of protecting and raising this helpless "creature" that she encountered.

While the plot might seem farfetched, this selfless trait is in fact similar to something that happened in real life at the Brookfield Zoo in Brookfield, Illinois. According to Wikipedia[xiv] in 1996 an 8-year-old female gorilla, named Binti Jua, selflessly rescued a 3-year-old boy who had fallen into the gorilla exhibit at the zoo. While onlookers screamed and panicked, Binti walked over to the unconscious boy, picked him up and cradled him, bringing him to safety within the enclosure until zoo personnel came to the rescue. The little boy suffered only a broken hand and a large gash on his face and Bindi was celebrated as a hero for her selfless act of animal altruism.

◆◆◆

About the Gorilla

Gorillas are social creatures who live in groups consisting of between 5 to 30 gorillas. Some additional details about the gorilla include:

- A group of gorillas is called a troop.
- Troop leaders (not the Girl Scout kind) are often the oldest male in the group, and there is usually only one adult male per troop.
- Troop leaders are determined by strength. Adult males compete for the troop leader title, with the strongest male being the winner.
- The leader of a gorilla troop is referred to as the silverback of the troop.
- The silverback's primary role is to protect the safety of the group. Their physical strength and power play a role in maintaining order, defending the group against potential threats, and asserting dominance.
- Silverbacks navigate complex social dynamics within the troop. They mediate conflicts, maintain order, and facilitate social interactions. Their ability to understand and manage relationships within the group is crucial for troop cohesion.
- Silverbacks also make decisions that impact the group, such as determining the direction of travel, selecting resting spots, or deciding when to forage. Their intelligence and leadership involve a degree of decision-making that affects the collective well-being of the troop.

◆◆◆

Leadership Lessons in Selflessness from the Gorilla

It's very easy to identify the silverback in every gorilla troop. They are bigger than the others in the troop and quite literally, have silver hair on their back. A few leadership lessons from the silverback include the following:

- In a gorilla troop, the dominant silverback often displays acts of selflessness by protecting and leading the group, **ensuring their safety**, and even sacrificing his own well-being for the sake of the troop. Like the gorilla, CARDINAL Leaders should also ensure the safety of their team... but in the business world, this takes the form of psychological safety. **Psychological safety** is the feeling of trust and confidence that CARDINAL Leaders create to selflessly allow their team to take the spotlight, share ideas, be vulnerable, and not be afraid to make mistakes or ask for help.

- Gorillas also symbolize selflessness due to their behavior within their social groups. They live in close-knit communities where they demonstrate care, protection, and **support for one another**. CARDINAL Leaders must also demonstrate support for their team by not only providing them with the training and tools they need to perform their jobs, but also by trusting and empowering them to make role-appropriate decisions that impact their daily tasks. Trusting others to do their jobs adequately requires the leader to selflessly release control over *everything* and be willing to support their employees "from the sidelines."

- Gorillas exhibit altruistic behaviors such as sharing food, providing comfort, and nurturing the young within their group. These actions highlight a sense of selflessness and care for the well-being of the community. CARDINAL Leaders must also selflessly **nurture the (professional) development and promotion of each of their employees.** You can always tell a true CARDINAL Leader, because they genuinely celebrate the growth of their team members and enjoy the success that their development brings to the team. One of the greatest accomplishments to a CARDINAL Leader is to see their team equipped with the knowledge and skills to perform their jobs autonomously and responsibly enough to get promoted and/or take the place of the CARDINAL Leader if they were to get promoted or move on. Ironically, it often does require the CARDINAL Leader to move on for their employees to get promoted or accept a leadership role themselves, because they are happy with their jobs and their leader and often don't <u>want</u> to move on. Never underestimate the power of working for a CARDINAL Leader!

◆◆◆

Interviewing for Selflessness

Another "hard to evaluate" trait that isn't typically included in the "Top 10" lists of common interview questions. When it comes to selflessness, you'll have to ask probing questions that require the candidate to elaborate on scenarios in which they demonstrate placing concern for others above concern for themselves. Below are a few suggestions.

Questions to ask:
1. What motivates you to help others?
2. Can you describe a time when you put the needs of your team above your own personal goals?
3. Tell me about a time when you had to handle a situation in which your own priorities conflicted with the needs of the team.
4. What is your definition of success?

Why these questions matter:

These questions can provide insight into whether the candidate has experience acting as a "servant leader," which is a philosophy in which the leader's *modus operandi* is to serve their people in a way that the team and the company thrives. Servant leadership isn't an "act" that our corporate peacocks can sustain for any period of time. So, these questions will be very telling.

What to look for:

Look for the candidate to provide answers that demonstrate their willingness to help others without expecting anything in return. You also want to listen for specific examples that provide clear evidence of experiences in which they prioritized others' needs over their own.

For example, I once led a project that required the use of a very detailed project plan that I had created specifically for that project. The client needed it to be in Excel and wanted to have massive amounts of minutia readily available in a format that was user friendly for the users of the tool, but aesthetically and visually appealing for the client to be able to follow along. I worked on it for hours to get it to a place where I felt it would serve the purposes that I needed to manage the dozens of deliverables being developed, each with a dozen or so milestones that had to be tracked over a very short timeframe.

Color coding, workflows, formulas, dropdown lists… this tool had it all, simply to make my life easier and the client happy. However, when I presented it to my team and explained the components that they were responsible for maintaining, they came back the next day and requested a modification that I knew would make my role a bit more complicated. But they outnumbered me, and I knew that the combined amount of time this modification would save *them* outweighed the small inconvenience it presented to *me*. So, I made the change for their benefit.

CARDINAL Leaders are more than willing to go the extra mile to help others, but you'll often find that their success stories tend to focus more on the success of others. In fact, their definition of success will most likely highlight the achievements of their team members and their pride in those achievements.

Red flags:

Because corporate peacocks most likely don't have personal experience acting selfless, don't be surprised if they struggle to provide you with detailed answers to these questions. Remember, they are self-centered so quite possibly will provide you with vague, "second-hand" stories (e.g., they witnessed THEIR boss doing something selfless and are plagiarizing that story for their own benefit) that don't include a lot of details.

Be diligent with asking probing, follow-up questions to their answers to help you ascertain whether they actually played the "lead role" in their own story.

◆◆◆

TL; DR Chapter 8: Selflessness & the Gorilla

- Gorillas are social animals who live in groups, called troops, that range in size from 5 to 30 gorillas. The leader of the troop is always a male silverback who is often the strongest and oldest male in the troop.
- The primary responsibility of the silverback is to ensure the safety of the troop. Like the gorilla, CARDINAL Leaders must ensure the *psychological* safety of their team by selflessly creating an atmosphere where their employees feel safe enough to take the spotlight, ask for help or make mistakes without fear of losing their jobs.
- Silverbacks selflessly make decisions that impact the group, such as determining the direction of travel, selecting resting spots, or deciding when to forage. CARDINAL Leaders also display selflessness by willingly supporting their team with the trust, tools, training, knowledge, and decision-making authority to effectively perform their jobs.
- Gorillas exhibit altruistic behaviors such as sharing food, providing comfort, and nurturing the young within their group. These actions highlight a sense of selflessness and care for the well-being of the community. CARDINAL Leaders selflessly nurture the *professional* development and promotion of each of their employees. They genuinely celebrate the growth of their team members and enjoy the success that their development contributes to the team.
- Incorporate my recommended questions in your interview process to evaluate selflessness with leadership candidates.

❖❖❖

CHAPTER 9: EMPATHY & THE ELEPHANT

*Definition of **Empathetic**: The psychological identification with the thoughts/feelings of others.*

The final and sixth trait of the six traits of a CARDINAL Leader is empathy. In the Ethology of Leaders, I've selected the elephant to represent this leadership characteristic all CARDINAL Leaders should possess. While some of the other traits in this book are represented symbolically, empathy in elephants has been observed to be a reality.

I personally have a level of empathy that, quite frankly, can be a burden. The physical pain that I feel when I see animals suffering is such that I avoid it at all costs. I even changed career choices as a child when I found out that veterinarians don't just get to hug and pet animals all day. Vets actually *have* to deal with sick and injured animals, and frequently <u>cause</u> animals pain when treating them. So, before the age of 10, I had already selected and retired from a career as a veterinarian. I'm so pathetically empathetic that I'm thankful even now when I have to take my pets to the vet for their shots, and the vet takes my pet "to the back" to give them their vaccinations.

❖❖❖

About the Elephant

A group of elephants can consist of up to 100 elephants. Elephants are highly social animals with a complex range of behaviors. A few more facts about the elephant:

- A group of elephants is most often called a herd.
- Adult male and female elephants live separately, except during mating season. While females live year-round in a herd, adult males are often more solitary.
- Elephant herds are matriarchal, so it's no surprise that their female leaders are known to demonstrate a great sense of empathy, calmness, togetherness, and determination.
- Herd leaders are typically the oldest females within the group, and it's their wisdom that leads the migration of their herd to ensure their survival according to food sources and seasons.
- While most herds are familial consisting of direct bloodlines of mothers, aunts, and sisters, herd matriarchs are naturally one of the most doting females of the herd whose intelligence and wisdom provide them with the knowledge and influence to naturally emerge as the herd leader.

◆ ◆ ◆

Leadership Lessons in Empathy from the Elephant

The elephant represents my favorite example of leadership in the animal kingdom. The fact that they can feel emotions and display empathy speaks to their high level of intelligence. A few more leadership lessons from the elephant include:

- Elephants are known to **engage in comforting behaviors**, such as using various vocalizations or the use of their trunks to touch and console other elephants displaying signs of distress. In my research, I ran across an organization in Kenya called The Sheldrick Wildlife Trust. According to their website, this amazing organization was established almost 50 years ago in 1977 to rescue baby elephants who had been orphaned due to poachers. In an article on the site titled, *The Making of a Matriarch*, the founder's daughter, Angela Sheldrick, explains that "… in the wild, baby elephants are raised in a cocoon of love. Mothers and nannies wrap their trunks around a calf's belly, over its shoulder, under its neck, often touching its mouth. It's a beautiful, joyful, communal affair — and these are all behaviors we also observe from the more maternal members of our orphan herd. It's as if they know that younger orphans thrive on tactile affection, and they provide it in abundance."[xv]

Important note: I absolutely am not encouraging leaders to touch their employees to comfort them! Instead, I'm saying that CARDINAL Leaders should be able to display empathy to comfort employees going through a difficult time. This is often a simple conversation between the leader and the employee to express their concern and ask if there's anything they can do to help.

- Elephants also display empathy through certain **celebrations**, such as when they've been reunited with a separated herd member, for example.

Elephants also have special celebrations they express when interacting with human caregivers. In 2023, a film called *The Elephant Whisperers* won an Oscar Award in the Best Documentary Short Film category. In this film, a tribal couple in India raise an orphaned baby elephant given into their care. A strong bond forms between the elephant and the couple, and includes some heartwarming celebrations exhibited by the baby elephant in response to his human caregivers. CARDINAL Leaders naturally "come to the table with" a routine of celebration rituals as well. Even something as simple as recognizing birthdays or work anniversaries at monthly team meetings or celebrating the successful completion of a project and highlighting the achievements of the team during a quarterly call are meaningful ways in which CARDINAL Leaders demonstrate empathy via celebrations that recognize their employees in meaningful ways. The sincerity with which these small doses of recognition really matter to employees and are important to the cohesion of the group.

- Another way in which elephants convey empathy is through the **cooperative care** of their calves. As Sheldrick pointed out earlier, raising calves in the herd is a communal affair. It's standard operating procedure for the adult females of the herd to participate in the care, protection, and rearing of the calves. Ironically, CARDINAL Leaders instinctively take on this approach as well with their co-workers and employees who aren't their direct reports. If there's a mentor program within an organization, you'll most likely find some CARDINAL Leaders there taking on mentees and providing professional development guidance and advice to perfect strangers within their organization.

I've personally been guilty of recognizing the talent and potential in some of my peers' direct reports and lamented their underutilization. I frequently led pilot projects within my department to experiment with new technology or processes to determine whether we should incorporate them into our infrastructure. Without fail, I would reach out to my peers to "borrow" one of their employees for the duration of the project so that my peer could have representation from their team on the project.

I cannot tell you the sheer joy I felt witnessing firsthand my peer's employees completely thrive on these projects. They were suddenly excited to show up for work each day, often working overtime against my "orders." They were finally able to tap into their creativity and ingenuity and exploit their skills in a way that highlighted their real potential. The projects also provided them with unprecedented visibility. Simply because they worked with someone who was empathetic and cared about them enough to present them with a stretch assignment that would get them out of their daily routine. I ran across a quote recently (I have no idea whom to attribute to); however, I felt compelled to conclude this section with it because it resonated with me so much:

> *People don't care how much you know unless they know how much you care.*

◆◆◆

Interviewing for Empathy

Empathy in a CARDINAL Leader is so critical that I could probably write an entire book on this characteristic alone. Surprisingly, empathy is another trait that isn't often included in the interview process. But if a leader doesn't have empathy for their own employees, imagine how they might treat their colleagues and/or clients?

Questions to ask:
1. Can you tell me about a time you used empathy to solve a problem?
2. What are your strengths and weaknesses in terms of emotional abilities?
3. How do you handle your employees' problems?
4. How do you deal with your anger?
5. What would you do if someone on your team seemed distracted and unable to do their job?

Why these questions matter:
By asking these interview questions, employers can gain a deeper understanding of a candidate's self-awareness regarding their empathetic abilities, which are essential for fostering collaboration, communication, and a positive workplace culture. These questions also demonstrate a candidate's ability to recognize emotional needs in others and take action.

What to look for:
Listen for answers that demonstrate the candidate's inclination to understand and support their colleagues during challenging times, reflecting their empathy and willingness to provide assistance. An empathetic candidate will convey a sense of fairness in their answers and a desire to solve problems in a way that doesn't alienate team members or place blame.

Red flags:

If a candidate's answers include blaming others, this is an immediate red flag. Effective conflict resolution requires awareness and concern for all parties involved. Corporate peacocks often see empathy as a weakness, and therefore might have difficulty answering these questions with any amount of enthusiasm. Remember, they're masterful imposters, so again, you'll need to listen for an undercurrent of indifference or negativity from them when answering these questions.

◆◆◆

TL; DR Chapter 9: Empathy & the Elephant

- A group of elephants is called a herd. Elephant herds are matriarchal, with the leader often being the oldest female of the group who is known to demonstrate a great sense of empathy, wisdom, calmness, togetherness, and determination. Male elephants are often more solitary and typically only interact with the herd during mating season.
- Elephants display empathy by consistently engaging in comforting behaviors with their herd. This can include comforting vocalizations or using their trunks to "embrace" herd members who are in distress. Important note: I absolutely am not encouraging leaders to touch their employees to comfort them! Instead, I'm saying that CARDINAL Leaders should be able to display empathy to comfort employees going through a difficult time. This is often a simple conversation between the leader and the employee to express their concern and ask if there's anything they can do to help.
- Elephants also display empathy via "celebration" rituals when they have cause to rejoice. Celebrating a herd member coming home after being separated from the group is one celebration activity that has been thoroughly observed and documented in the elephant herd. CARDINAL Leaders can't help but incorporate celebrations into their work routines because they genuinely enjoy highlighting others' success and achievements. Even something as simple as a monthly team call or newsletter in which the CARDINAL Leader celebrates an employee's birthday, work anniversary, promotion or successful completion of a project is a healthy way to display empathy and ensure that every employee is recognized at some point throughout the year.
- Female elephants are known for the cooperative care they express for one another and for the herd's offspring. It's standard operating procedure

for the adult females of the herd to participate in the care, protection, and rearing of the calves. CARDINAL Leaders also instinctively take this approach as well with their co-workers and employees who aren't their direct reports. If there's a mentor program within an organization, you'll most likely find some CARDINAL Leaders there taking on mentees and providing professional development guidance and advice to perfect strangers within their organization.
- Incorporate my recommended questions in your interview process to evaluate empathy with leadership candidates.

❖❖❖

CHAPTER 10: YOUR ACTION PLAN FOR LEADERSHIP REFORM

"Inspire the best in others. You'll never be disappointed."

-- Me – The DIY Leader

If you've made it this far in the book, I'm fairly certain you are (or have the potential to be) a CARDINAL Leader. Corporate peacocks most likely abandoned reading this book at the first sign of "emotion."

Now that you know the ethology of a CARDINAL Leader, the type of traits that you should be looking for when selecting your leaders, and even interview questions you can ask to hire CARDINAL Leaders… let's take a look at the action plan for implementing Leadership Reform in your organization.

CARDINAL Leaders are the foundation to Leadership Reform and the conduit of your company's transformation to eliminate toxic bosses and bullying in the workplace and increase employee engagement, productivity, and profits. If the only thing you take from this book is how to hire and/or promote better (CARDINAL) Leaders, then I'd call that a win. No doubt, that step alone can transform an organization, which is why I spent the majority of this book detailing the characteristics specific to this amazing breed of leader.

Following is a simple action plan to successfully carry out Leadership Reform in your organization.

◆◆◆

Ground Zero: Establish Your Pack by Starting at the Top

Transformation of this sort starts at the top of the food chain. For an organization to turn itself around and use this methodology to increase the bottom line, increase profits, increase employee engagement, and decrease turnover, this type of change has to be a top-down initiative. Unfortunately, this is not a formula that will be successful long-term if it doesn't have support from the C-Suite. Even getting buy in from HR to update their hiring practices for people leaders requires executive sponsorship.

While Leadership Reform may seem like a heavy lift that will require years to implement, I'm here to tell you that isn't necessarily the case IF you have support from the C-Suite. Therefore, before you even move to the next step in this process, assemble a strong team of champions who can help you create a compelling narrative that the C-Suite can't refuse.

When I first embarked on this mission, I immediately started reaching out on social media to perfect strangers. I looked for like-minded people who were not only passionate about this topic, but also had expertise in areas that I didn't. I "became the wolf" and HUMBLED myself to perfect strangers to pitch my mission and ask for their support. It is through this group of amazing, passionate, selfless, empathetic people that I was able to assemble the content, resources, and data I needed to formulate and document this methodology for Leadership Reform.

So, while I'd like to pontificate about the story of my pack for multiple chapters, I've been advised that I'm "losing the plot" a bit. However, I cannot proceed without emphasizing the "power of the pack" to help demonstrate that even perfect strangers can and will help you if you are simply brave enough to ask. There is no excuse why you can't do the same within your own organization to assemble a powerful team of people who are passionate enough about

Leadership Reform to help you campaign for the cause with the C-Suite and other leaders.

My Leadership Reform Pack Members

Here is a little bit of information about the amazingly talented people who helped me on my journey to "make the world a better place, one leader at a time." These folks joined me on my Leadership Reform podcast series, courtesy of Terry McDougall (details below) to speak about workplace bullying and toxic leaders. The entire 6-part series is available on my website www.leadershipreno.com and YouTube channel at youtube.com/@thediyleader.

Every single one of these awe-inspiring folks responded positively to a pitch from this perfect stranger. They willingly took time out of their busy schedules to support the cause and I'm forever grateful for THEIR leadership, expertise, and dedication to this cause. They have all been fighting this fight much longer than I have and I know have personally changed many lives with their compassion and diligence.

1. **Tomas Chamorro-Premuzic, Ph.D.: Psychologist, author & entrepreneur**: I ran across Dr. Tomas' TEDx Talk based on his book, *Why Do So Many Incompetent Men Become Leaders (and How to Fix It)?* and it's still one of my favorite TEDx Talks to this day. "Dr. Tomas," as he is known, is an international authority in leadership assessment, people analytics, and talent management. He's the Chief Talent Scientist at ManpowerGroup and professor of business psychology at both University College London and Columbia University. At the time of this writing, Dr. Tomas has written 11 books and over 150 scientific papers on the psychology of talent, leadership, innovation, and AI. His latest book, released in 2023, in fact focuses on AI and is titled, *I, Human: AI, Automation, and the Quest to Reclaim What Makes Us Unique.* His commercial work focuses on the creation of science-based tools that improve organizations' ability to predict performance, and people's ability to understand themselves. Dr. Tomas' work supplied me with the hard data that quantified the traits of an effective leader and the explanation for why toxic bosses are so prevalent in our society today. In my pack, Dr. Tomas became my "statistician." His immense amount of research and data established unbiased conclusions that gave validation to my instincts about leadership. You can visit his personal website at www.drtomas.com.

2. **Amy C. Edmondson, Ph.D.**: Dr. Amy is a Novartis Professor of Leadership & Management at Harvard Business School, author of several books, the latest of which was released in 2023 and is titled, *The Right Kind of Wrong: The Science of Failing Well*. She's also co-author of *Extreme Teaming*; author of dozens of related articles and a multiple TED Talks/TEDx Talk presenter. Dr. Amy has done extensive research that examines psychological safety and teaming within and between organizations and is particularly interested in how leaders enable the learning and collaboration that are vital to performance in a dynamic environment. Ironically, the fact that Dr. Amy and I share a last name is what helped me get my foot in the door with her. I'm fairly certain she thought I was a long-lost relative of hers that she hadn't spoken to in a while. So, she responded to my "blind DM." Of course, we then connected over a shared passion for leadership, psychological safety in the workplace, and eradicating workplace bullies via better leaders. Dr. Amy's personal website is www.amycedmondson.com.

3. **Kalyani Pardeshi:** Kalyani was my very first "soul sister" connection on LinkedIn, and she is still one of my favorite people to this day. Kalyani and I bonded over our shared experiences as targets of bullying in the workplace, plus our passion for helping others avoid the same. Kalyani is a TEDx Talk speaker, award-winning author of the book *Unbullied*, a Quantum Human Design specialist who has dedicated her career to eradicating bullies of all ages, and a recently Certified Flowcess instructor. Visit Kalyani's website at www.kalyanispeaks.com.

4. **Deb Falzoi:** Deb is another one of those selfless people put on this earth to help make the world a better place. She's the founder and owner of Dignity Together and has dedicated years of her life to pushing for legislation to combat bullying in the workplace. Deb works tirelessly on behalf of those who have been bullied to provide them with coaching, counseling, and training resources to educate and heal targets of workplace bullying. She "talks soft but carries a big stick." Her website, podcast, and newsletter are full of information and events to support people who have been bullied in the workplace. Deb is a wealth of knowledge, and quickly became my anti-bullying "legislation" expert. Visit her website at www.dignitytogether.org.

5. **Terry B. McDougall:** Terry is an executive and career coach, speaker, and best-selling author of the book, *Winning the Game of Work: Career Happiness and Success on Your Own Terms*. Terry has extensive experience with hosting and guesting on podcasts. A quick chat with her convinced me that she was the one who could help bring my "podcast panel" vision to life. As with many of the people in my pack, Terry had also been personally bullied at work and her passion, plus 30 years of corporate business experience (15 of which were in senior managerial roles), led her to become a certified coach and concentrate on helping leaders step fully into their potential to lead satisfying careers. She works with managers, executives, and professionals who want to draw upon their greatest, most authentic abilities to positively impact their organizations. She supports clients who are creating change, driving innovation, and navigating transitions. Visit Terry's website to learn more at www.terrybmcdougall.com.

6. **Alexander N. Andrews:** Alex and I met via a random "Social Saturday" event on LinkedIn and hit it off immediately. Within just a few days of meeting, we had scheduled a call to chat and learn more about one another. This was no small feat because Alex lives in Australia! I found Alex to be "the male equivalent of me" and during our very first chat, we bonded over our shared experiences with bullying. Most importantly, Alex's background was similar to mine in that he used his bad experience of being bullied to instead become a great leader to others. Based on his personal experience as a successful leader with a career spanning 30 years, Alex also wrote a book, titled *UNLIKE A BOSS*, in which he shares his experiences with some leadership horror stories he personally witnessed/was subjected to and describes how he overcame them to build highly engaged teams. Our leadership philosophies are so similar, in fact, that I refused to finish reading *his* book until I finished mine... simply because we speak the same language, and I didn't want to be accused of plagiarism. Learn more about his book at www.unlikeaboss.com.au.

Eight brilliant people, whom I met via LinkedIn, were able to collaborate, strategize, schedule, plan, and record six podcast sessions in a matter of months. If I can assemble this elite pack of strangers in that amount of time, there's no excuse why you shouldn't be able to quickly assemble your own Leadership Reform pack within your organization.

Figure 10-1: My Leadership Reform Pack

❖ ❖ ❖

Step 1: Implement Employee Engagement Surveys

Now that you have your Leadership Reform pack, your next step is to objectively identify the problem people in your flock. If I've convinced you that CARDINAL Leaders are your secret weapon to profits, then you must realize the opposite is also true. Toxic bosses and corporate peacocks are a virus that can infiltrate an organization and bring it to its knees impacts them from the inside out. Therefore, you have to identify those people and perform an intervention. For an organization to perform this level of introspection, you're going to need help.

As I mentioned at the beginning of this book, identifying toxic bosses can be done by evaluating employee turnover patterns and employee engagement survey results. If you do not currently conduct annual employee engagement surveys... you need to start. This is an important investment that will not only reveal the weakest links amongst your leadership population but will also serve the purpose of providing your employees with "a voice." This matters because it demonstrates to employees that your organization has empathy and that you care about their opinion.

> **No.1**
>
> **Employee Engagement Surveys**
>
> Invest in implementing (or properly leveraging) Employee Engagement Surveys to evaluate the health of your company, according to your employees.
>
> Take action on results.

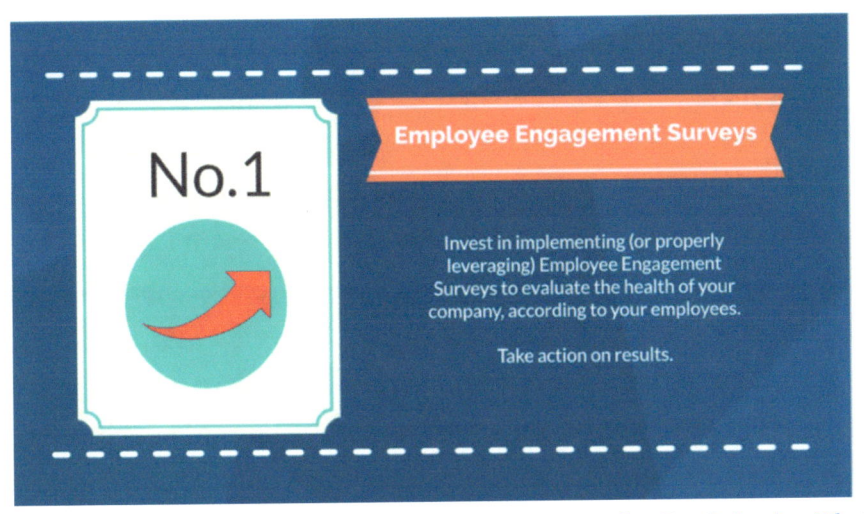

Figure 10-2: From the course, [Leadership Reno: How to Select People Leaders Who Will Drive Your Business Forward](#).

Generally speaking, employees do not trust your HR department when it comes to filing grievances. Regardless of how amazing your HR personnel are at their jobs; history reveals time and again that their loyalty in any bullying situation is to the company that signs their paychecks. Hence the need for a third-party assessor for implementing employee engagement surveys. Even though you are also paying this third party, their reputation is dependent on their honesty and accuracy. There are numerous, reputable organizations, such as Gallup, who can effectively perform an impartial evaluation and provide consultation to help you take action on the results.

It can take years for an organization to prove to employees that their anonymous feedback on these surveys will remain anonymous and will not be used against them. So, don't assume that high scores resulting from these surveys in the beginning means that your company doesn't have any issues and therefore you can go back to business as usual. High scores first time out of the gate on these surveys can sometimes be the result of employees answering questions in a way they believe won't get them in trouble if the answers are mapped back to them. Employee engagement surveys are most valuable when you have year-over-year statistics that can be compared and reported on with each survey.

A word of caution about employee engagement surveys: until employees trust that they can answer the survey questions without fear of repercussion, the results even for toxic leaders might not paint a true picture. Companies tend to push leaders to get 100% of their employees to take the survey. After all, the more employees who complete the survey, the more powerful the resulting data. However, toxic bosses can turn this directive into a "competition" where the "winner" is awarded some sort of prize or recognition. This can subsequently force employees to take the survey even if they are uncomfortable with it. As a result, their answers will most likely not reflect their honest feelings. So don't be surprised if your toxic bosses and corporate peacocks have a 100% response rate with fairly impressive scores at first.

Again, taking advantage of the third-party assessor to help your organization interpret the results will provide you with your best chance at a successful implementation and help mitigate employees who might still be a bit suspicious about answering the survey questions with complete honesty.

◆◆◆

Step 2: Modify Your Standards for Hiring People Leaders

Carefully selecting empathetic, authentic, and humble people leaders who inspire the best in others is the easiest and single-most impactful business decision organizations have control over. Incorporate the questions I've provided in this book to evaluate for these important traits throughout the interview process to ensure that you're selecting CARDINAL Leaders who will transform your business by decreasing turnover and increasing employee engagement and profits. These questions should apply to interviewing for all people-leader roles, at all levels of the organization.

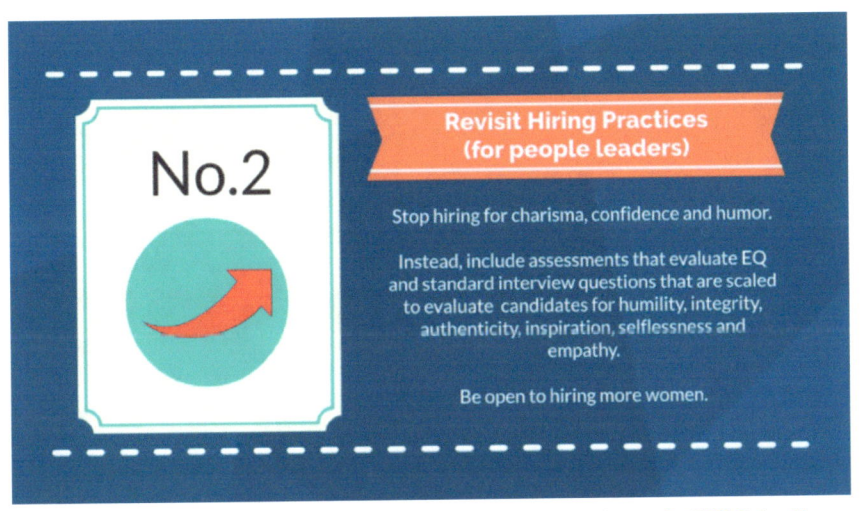

No.2

Revisit Hiring Practices (for people leaders)

Stop hiring for charisma, confidence and humor.

Instead, include assessments that evaluate EQ and standard interview questions that are scaled to evaluate candidates for humility, integrity, authenticity, inspiration, selflessness and empathy.

Be open to hiring more women.

Figure 10-3: [Leadership Reno: How to Select People Leaders Who Will Drive Your Business Forward](#).

◆◆◆

Step 3: Revise the Performance Metrics for your People Leaders

Now that you've implemented employee engagement surveys, incorporate those scores in your leader's annual reviews. Hold them accountable! While you're at it, include employee turnover metrics in their performance reviews as well. CARDINAL Leaders are not scared of either of these numbers.

Toxic bosses and corporate peacocks, however, will struggle with this level of scrutiny and will make their opinion known. They'll have an excuse for each of the "poor performers" on their team who left the company under their charge. They'll also have an explanation for any low employee engagement scores. Relying on these metrics and identifying patterns will paint an irrefutable picture that will enable you to remain objective.

Revisit Performance Metrics (for people leaders)

No.3

Include Employee Engagement survey results as a metric that leaders are held accountable for in their annual reviews.

Include employee turnover as a metric for people leaders.

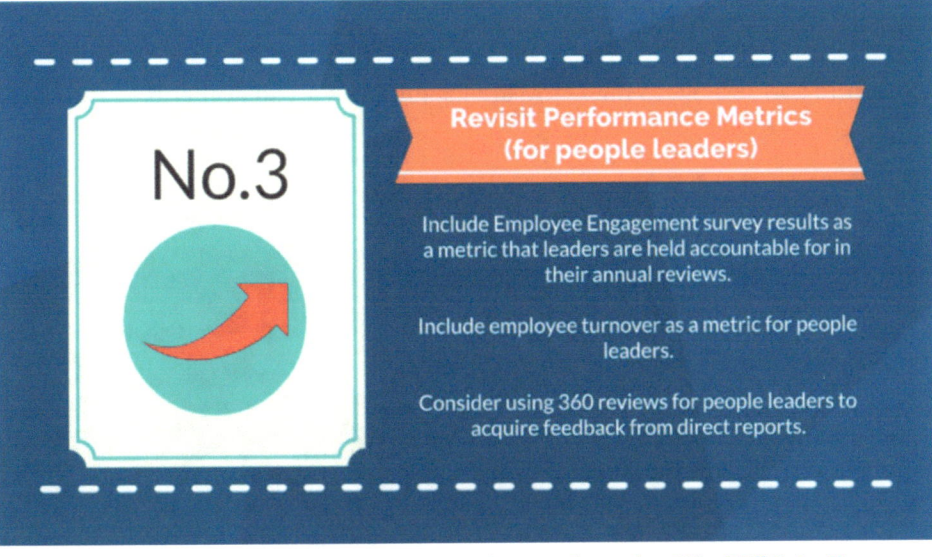

Consider using 360 reviews for people leaders to acquire feedback from direct reports.

Figure 10-4: [Leadership Reno: How to Select People Leaders Who Will Drive Your Business Forward](#).

❖❖❖

Step 4: Rehome, Rehabilitate or Retrain your Toxic Bosses

This is the most important step in this formula... because all of the employee surveys and bad reviews in the world are meaningless if you don't take action on the results!

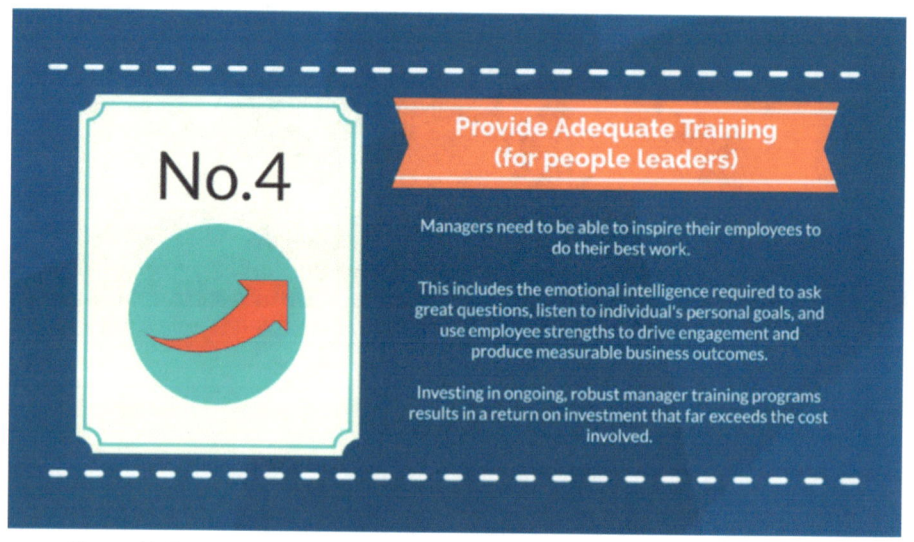

No.4

Provide Adequate Training (for people leaders)

Managers need to be able to inspire their employees to do their best work.

This includes the emotional intelligence required to ask great questions, listen to individual's personal goals, and use employee strengths to drive engagement and produce measurable business outcomes.

Investing in ongoing, robust manager training programs results in a return on investment that far exceeds the cost involved.

Figure 10-5: From the course, [Leadership Reno: How to Select People Leaders Who Will Drive Your Business Forward.](#)

If your toxic bosses survive the first three steps of this program, there's hope. These might be your misled, misunderstood, or just poorly trained people leaders of the world who can be rehabilitated and retrained to become the type of leader who inspires the best in others. It will take work though, and a lot of training. Those who survive the process deserve to be rewarded. Give them the fancy title, the great project, or that healthy raise and/or bonus. They deserve it.

And remember, for every one of their employees who increases their engagement (and therefore productivity) because this leader has "turned a new leaf" and the employees now enjoy working for them, you've just saved yourself one-third of the payroll on that leader's team. Remember our simple formula from earlier in this book:

- Six employees @ $70,000 each = $420,000 annual team payroll
- Divided by a third, = $140,000 saved in turnover costs per year

By rehabilitating that leader and avoiding any of those six employees leaving, that leader has literally just "saved" (some may even say "earned") you $140,000 that year! Simply by not being an ass. And that doesn't even account for the increase in those employees' productivity.

Your organization will literally transform before your eyes with the right people leaders in place. They're hard to find, but my suggestion is to start by taking a peek at their LinkedIn profile, Recommendations section. Look for recommendations from people who are direct reports of that person. CARDINAL Leaders have the type of relationship with their employees that makes this a common practice in their world.

If you don't see any recommendations from former employees of a people leader… ask yourself why? Could they be hiding something? Do YOU have recommendations on LinkedIn from former employees? If not, why? If you do though, I'd venture to say that you're simply reading this book for pleasure. Because you clearly already "get it."

❖❖❖

TL; DR Chapter 10: Your Action Plan for Leadership Reform

- Step 0: Establish your pack. Transformation of this sort starts at the top. This type of initiative must have the support from the C-Suite to be successful. So, assemble a pack of Leadership Reform champions to help you gain executive support.
- Step 1: Implement employee engagement surveys. Use a third-party firm to implement these surveys and evaluate the results. Not only are you showing your employees you care by giving them a voice, but you're also able to identify problem areas in the organization that you might not have otherwise noticed.
- Step 2: Modify your standards for hiring people leaders. Incorporate questions into your interview process that enable you to assess the EQ of your leadership candidates. Then, hire more CARDINAL Leaders!
- Step 3: Revise the metrics for which you evaluate your people leaders. Incorporate people metrics (such as employee engagement scores and turnover) in leader's annual reviews. If they're doing this right, their sales and productivity numbers will follow.
- Step 4: Rehome and/or rehabilitate your toxic bosses. Immediately. Get them out of the role of people leader. They're most likely intelligent and have some great ideas, so could be great for strategic, individual contributor roles. But keep them away from your employees… or rehabilitate the ones who seem to actually have a heart.

◆◆◆

CONCLUSION

There you have it. As promised, I've provided you with a compelling case for Leadership Reform, including a simple formula for selecting the right people leaders to *increase* employee engagement, production, and revenue, and *decrease* employee turnover. You now:

- Know the characteristics we should all be looking for when hiring, promoting, and evaluating people leaders.
- Understand the consequences of *not* making Leadership Reform a priority in your organization.
- Possess a high-level action plan for implementing Leadership Reform in your workplace.

I'd like to wrap up this book with a simple quote. Of course, it just so happens that it comes from a movie with animals, but it's relevant here because it speaks about courage.

In 2011, Matt Damon starred in the movie, *We Bought a Zoo*. This movie was based on the book of the same name and recounts the true story of Benjamin Mee and his two children as they struggle to move forward after the death of their beloved wife and mother.

Here's what he said:

> *"You know, sometimes all you need is 20 seconds of courage. Just literally, 20 seconds of just embarrassing bravery, and I promise you, something great will come of it."*
>
> *– Benjamin Mee – We Bought a Zoo*

Mee says this line when explaining how he met his children's mother. His courageous 20 seconds resulted in him meeting a girl, asking her out, falling in love, getting married, and having his two kids.

For some folks, that 20 seconds of courage could lead to you presenting a TEDx Talk, writing your own book, or hosting a podcast. Or it could lead you to a successful career doing something you never thought you'd be doing but waking up every day excited about "going to work." It could also lead to you meeting some great people, making lifelong friends, finding an unexpected business partner or even your soul mate.

But sometimes, that 20 seconds could be the beginning of a ripple effect that results in an increase in your company's bottom line, an increase in employee engagement, a reinvigoration of your company culture, and a decrease in toxic bosses.

The only thing I can't provide to you in this book is courage. Courage to just take 20 seconds to pitch the cause for Leadership Reform in your workplace. And I promise you, something great will come of it.

My sincerest thanks to all of you! Good luck. You got this.

Lisa

◆◆◆

About the Author

Lisa Edmondson

Lisa is an animal lover and a reading "addict," capitalizing on her Amazon Prime subscription and Kindle to read at least two books a week. She is also oddly obsessed with Colson Baker (a.k.a. Machine Gun Kelly). She loves to write and hopes to write his entrepreneurial story with him someday.

Lisa lives in Atlanta with her husband, Eric, and beloved cats, Quinn, Jasper, and Gunner. Her dream is to win the lottery someday so that she can live on the beach, open an animal rescue compound, and afford to hire enough people to take care of the animals, while she assumes the role of Chief Animal Hugger. The Ethology of Leaders is her first book.

◆◆◆

Acknowledgements

In addition to my family and the people of my "Leadership Reform pack" already listed in this book, there are a lot of other people whom I'd like to thank for getting me to this point in my life.

First up, that wonderful team of employees with whom I worked who made me the type of leader that I've written about in this book. The team "formerly known as Team Lisa." You all hold a very special place in my heart. Thank you to Jennifer Yench, Kris Thayer, Martha Baytos, Daniel Die, Maria Daley, Darla Edge, Reena Patel, Laura O'Shea, Sue Liwanag, Carene Kulis, Michael Davis, Fran Pierskalla, Ila Burrell, and Mary Jacobson. I'd also like to thank some former co-workers who were honorary members of my team, some of whom I hired, mentored, worked for or worked with very closely: Terri Maske, Jen Doyle, Andrea Myers, Janet Moore, Adrianna DiNenno, Chris Terrill, Gwynne McCartney, Lori Fleming, Toni Pennell, Liz Fretz, Sharmala Sharvanandan, Sarah Schiller, Laura Tait, Chris Clark, Maristella Pereira-Viana, Melissa Kruminas, Pam Schultz, Marilyn Sizemore, Glen Lexing, Michelle Gibson, Claudia Becker, Evelyn Moore, Allison Smith-Copeland, Wendy Flynn, Paul Despres, Brenda White, Amy Murzell, Jo Nordeen, Paul Karker, Sam McNair, Brittany Rancourt, Julianna Nemeth, Victoria Cleven, Shannon Herman, Web Bromley, Ari Devin, Alessandro Salvetti, and many others.

Next are the amazing people whom I met via LinkedIn, and whom I now consider dear friends. There are so many of you, so please accept my apologies if I missed anyone, but each of these folks have given me advice and/or cheered me on in some way that helped get me through my "year of discovery" and continue to have a positive impact on my life: Shani Anderson, Susannah Dawn, Cindi Cohn, Zahra Kabiri-Hendi, Stephen Eng, Elizabeth Ho, Alex Rainey, Chason Forehand, Mike Phillips, Calvin Lawrence, Trevor van Woerden, Daniel Knight,

Kelly Nelson, Nathan Hill, Colin Stevenson, Sandra J. Wilson, Jamie Edwards, Christopher S. Sellers, Nausheen I. Chen, Cat Smiley, Dr. Nupi Arora, Fihmiya Hamdan, Michael Drey, Amanda Goudeau, Julie Morey, Jules McVey, Julie Nester (The Three Julie's), Joseph Sutton, Gretchen Skalka, Tara LaFon Gooch, and "The League of Legendary Creators" (you know who you are).

I'd also like to thank two of the "OGs" who first introduced me to the world of instructional design. These are the folks who were part of the training department that I stumbled into as my first job after college. I still stay in touch with these two and went on to get my 2nd and 3rd jobs in the training realm due to my direct connections with them: Kathleen Stout and Leigh Anne Lankford. Not only did these ladies take me "under their wing" and introduce me to my career, but they also represent the type of CARDINAL Leader described in this book.

And then there's Jenna Irving. Jenna is another member of what I call, the "LinkedIn Class of 2022," and someone whom I am extremely grateful to have run across. Jenna is a published author in her own right. We met because I randomly ran across her posts in LinkedIn, and her advice and sense of humor resonated with me. Therefore, I become a frequent "Commentor" on her posts. We then bonded over our unapologetic usage of exclamation points, and loathing for bad people in the world. I think she might be my spirit animal, but more importantly, she was an editor for this book. Her advice and experience were instrumental in getting this book "over the finish line," and I will forever be in her debt for taking a chance on me and this project.

Lastly, I'd like to mention the other GREAT leader who had a huge impact on me and my career, Angela Fletcher. Angela is no longer with us, but she had a passion for leadership that I know would have landed her on TV and in the history books if her life was not cut short by cancer. I know she would be proud of me for writing this book, and hope I represented her well, by proxy. She taught me the art of leading with grace. No other leader I have ever encountered has been able to lead with the grace that she demonstrated in every situation. I wish she were still here so I could have sought her guidance when authoring this book. I know it would have been much better with her input. Regardless, I still speak to her "in my mind", and I know she's keeping an eye on me and cheering me on.

◆◆◆

Endnotes

[i] [Gallup] Gallup. 2023. *State of the Global Workplace: 2022 Report.* Accessed 2023. https://www.gallup.com/workplace/349484/state-of-the-global-workplace.aspx.

[ii] (University of Oxford 2019) University of Oxford. 2019. "News > Happy workers are 13% more productive." *University of Oxford.* October 24. Accessed October 2023. https://www.ox.ac.uk/news/2019-10-24-happy-workers-are-13-more-productive.

[iii] (Gallup 2023) Gallup. —. 2023. *The Benefits of Employee Engagement.* January 7. Accessed October 30, 2023. https://www.gallup.com/workplace/236927/employee-engagement-drives-growth.aspx.

[iv] (Gallup 2023)

[v] (Gerry Valentine 2018) Gerry Valentine, Former Forbes Council Member. 2018. *Executive Presence: What Is It, Why You Need It, And How To Get It.* July 31. Accessed January 30, 2023. https://www.forbes.com/sites/forbescoachescouncil/2018/07/31/executive-presence-what-is-it-why-you-need-it-and-how-to-get-it/?sh=be6cc5f6bc7f.

[vi] (Zuckerman 2020) Zuckerman, Arthur. 2020. *37 LEADERSHIP STATISTICS: 2020/2021 DATA, TRENDS & PREDICTIONS.* May 29. Accessed April 2022. https://comparecamp.com/leadership-statistics/.

[vii] Audubon. 2023. *Audubon > Guide to North American Birds > Northern Cardinal.* Accessed October 2023. https://www.audubon.org/field-guide/bird/northern-cardinal.

[viii] (Wikipedia 2023) Wikipedia. 2023. *Emotional Intelligence.* October 19. Accessed October 27, 2023. https://en.wikipedia.org/wiki/Emotional_intelligence.

[ix] (HR Research Institute 2018) HR Research Institute. 2018. *HR.com: The State of Employee Engagement in 2018: Leverage leadership and culture to maximize engagement.* March. Accessed 2023. https://www.hr.com/en/resources/free_research_white_papers/the-state-of-employee-engagement-in-2018-mar2018_jeqfvgoq.html.

[x] (Percy 2022) Percy, Sally. 2022. *Eight Leadership Lessons From Dogs.* April 11. Accessed November 8, 2023. https://www.forbes.com/sites/sallypercy/2022/04/11/eight-leadership-lessons-from-dogs/?sh=1ed905e856ad.

[xi] (Julie Choi 2019) Julie Choi, Former Forbes Councils Member. 2019. *Leadership: Three Questions to Unlock Authenticity at Work.* January 9. Accessed November 11, 2023. https://www.forbes.com/sites/forbeshumanresourcescouncil/2019/01/09/three-questions-to-unlock-authenticity-at-work/?sh=48a26d823404.

[xii] (Edmondson 2023) Edmondson, Amy C. 2023. *Amazon > Right Kind of Wrong.* October 24. Accessed December 2, 2023. https://www.amazon.com/Right-Kind-Wrong-Edmondson-Amy-ebook/dp/B0CLRTDBTM/ref=sr_1_1?crid=361GF3Z49M8DF&keywords=the+right+kind+of+wrong+amy&qid=1701549466&s=books&sprefix=the+right+kind+o%2Cstripbooks%2C77&sr=1-1.

[xiii] (Open ai) OpenAI. 2023. *GPT-3.5-based AI Language Model.* December 2. Accessed December 2, 2023. https://www.openai.com/.

[xiv] (Wikipedia 2023) Binti Jua Wikipedia. 2023. *Binti Jua.* December 3. Accessed December 3, 2023. https://en.wikipedia.org/wiki/Binti_Jua.

[xv] (Sheldrick 2020) Sheldrick, Angela. 2020. *The Makings of a Matriarch.* April 30. Accessed December 3, 2023. https://www.sheldrickwildlifetrust.org/news/fieldnotes/makings-of-a-matriarch.

◆◆◆

Made in the USA
Columbia, SC
15 January 2024

The Ethology of Leaders

How to Leverage Leadership Lessons from the Animal Kingdom to be a GREAT Leader of People (and Increase Profits)!

Lisa Edmondson

Leadership Reno, LLC